LE PETIT PLET

Anglo-Norman Text Society
No. XX
(for 1962)

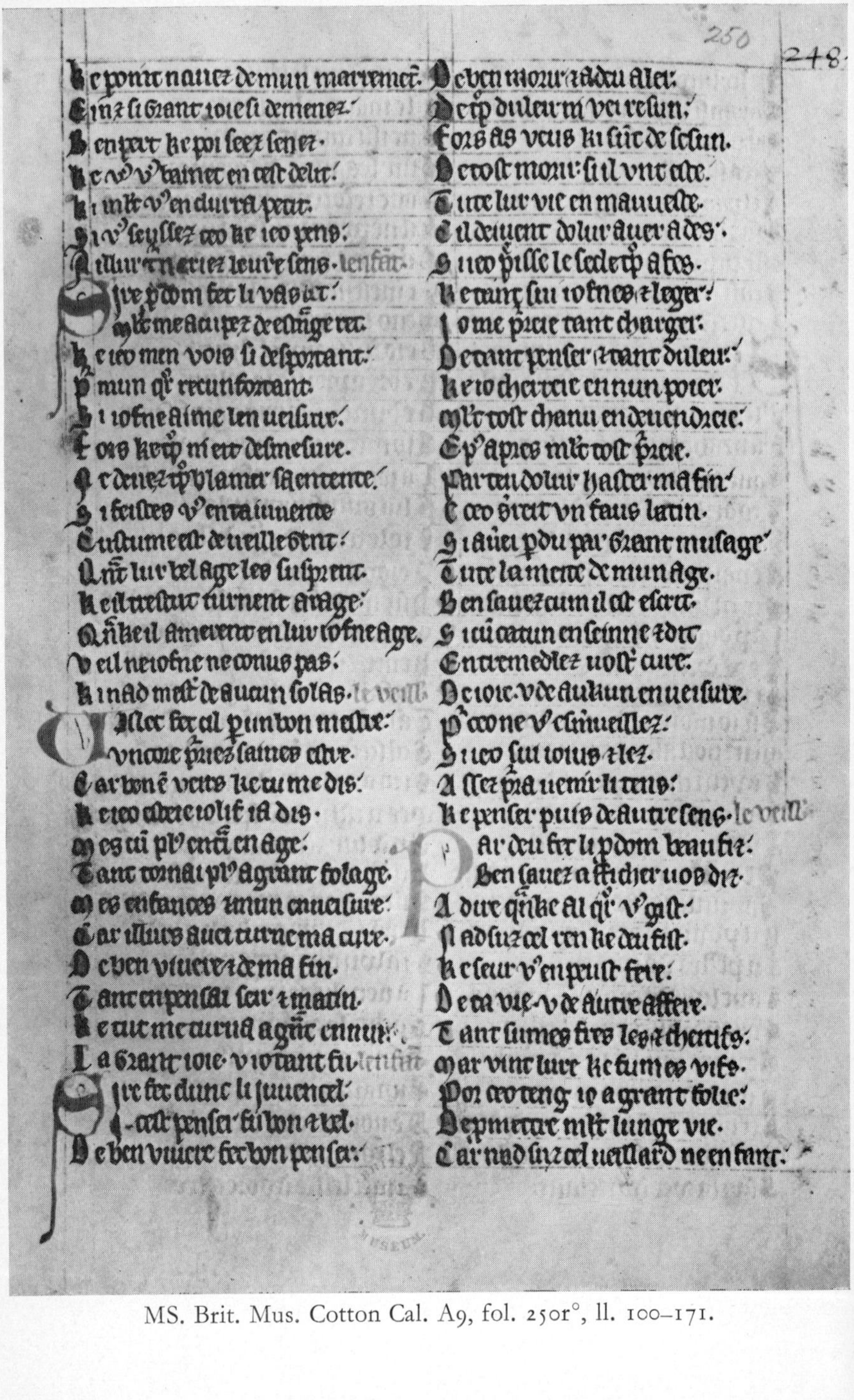

MS. Brit. Mus. Cotton Cal. A9, fol. 250r°, ll. 100–171.

ANGLO-NORMAN TEXTS—XX

LE PETIT PLET

Edited by

BRIAN S. MERRILEES

OXFORD

Published for the ANGLO-NORMAN TEXT SOCIETY
by BASIL BLACKWELL
1970

631   11990   6

Library of Congress Catalog Card No.: 69-20436

Printed in Great Britain by Alden & Mowbray Ltd
at the Alden Press, Oxford
and bound at Kemp Hall Bindery

THIS work has been published with the help of a grant from the Humanities Research Council of Canada using funds provided by the Canada Council.

PREFACE

THE existence of the *Petit Plet* was first indicated in 1800 by the Abbé de la Rue[1] in a discussion of two other poems, the *Vie de seint Josaphaz* and the *Set Dormanz*, both by an Anglo-Norman poet Chardri. To this same Chardri the Abbé de la Rue ascribed the *Petit Plet*, a view that no one since has seen any reason to contradict. Numerous allusions to the poem and its three manuscripts were made by early nineteenth-century scholars, but it was not until 1834 that part of the text was printed. Adelbert von Keller's *Romvart*[2] reproduced the first 366 lines of the Vatican manuscript and the last 13 lines of the *Petite Philosophie*,[3] wrongly believing them to be part of the same poem. Forty-five years later, the German medievalist, John Koch, published the complete works of Chardri as the first volume of the *Altfranzösische Bibliothek* series.[4]

Koch's edition, based on all manuscripts, contains detailed studies of language and versification as well as material on the sources, date and author. However, a satisfactory glossary is lacking, Koch having been content to draw up a short list of rare words whose meanings are given in the notes, while the text itself is an attempted reconstruction of an original, mainly from his base MS., Brit. Mus. Cotton Cal. A9. His regularizing procedures, besides confusing the linguistic picture, lead him at times to gloss over difficulties which deserve comment and his notes, which are included with the variants, do not take account of many textual problems and references.

In the present edition I have as far as possible followed the Cotton manuscript and the few departures from it are noted clearly at the foot of each page. A selective glossary has been included and new material added to the sections on sources and to the critical notes. The linguistic sections remain substantially the same as in Koch's edition with a change of presentation and emphasis. A table of proverbs has been added.

In the preparation of this work, begun at the suggestion of Prof.

---

[1] *Archaeologia* 13 (London, 1800), 234.
[2] Mannheim, 1834; Paris, 1844; cf. Introduction, p. xv.
[3] Ed. W. H. Trethewey (Chicago, 1939); reprinted by the A.N.T.S. as the first volume in this series (Oxford, 1939).
[4] *Chardry's 'Josaphaz, Set Dormanz und Petit Plet'* (Heilbronn, 1879).

Dominica Legge, I have received generous help from many teachers, colleagues and friends to whom go my sincere thanks. I am particularly indebted to two people, Professor R.-L. Wagner who so ably directed my research in Paris and Professor T. B. W. Reid whose guidance in preparing this edition for publication has been invaluable.

Victoria College,
Toronto, 1968

CONTENTS

PREFACE vii

ABBREVIATIONS AND SHORT TITLES x

INTRODUCTION xi

    Title xi

    The Manuscripts xi

        Abbreviations and Accents xv

        Manuscript Filiation xvi

    Language xviii

        A. Phonology xviii

        B. Morphology xx

          1. Declension xx

          2. Conjugation xxii

        C. Syntax xxiv

        D. Versification xxvii

    Author xxviii

    Date xxxii

    Sources xxxiii

    Establishment of the Text xxxv

TEXT 1

NOTES 59

TABLE OF PROVERBS 74

GLOSSARY 76

INDEX OF PROPER NAMES 86

ABBREVIATIONS AND SHORT TITLES

A.N.T.S.   Anglo-Norman Text Society.

E.E.T.S.   Early English Text Society.

F.E.W.   W. von Wartburg, *Französisches Etymologisches Wörterbuch* (Bonn-Leipzig-Basel, 1922–).

Gdf.   F. Godefroy, *Dictionnaire de l'ancienne langue française*, 10 vols. (Paris, 1880–1902).

Koch   *Chardry's 'Josaphaz, Set Dormanz und Petit Plet'*, Altfranzösische Bibliothek 1 (Heilbronn, 1879).

Morawski   J. Morawski, *Proverbes français antérieurs au XVe siècle*, Classiques français du moyen âge 47 (Paris, 1925).

Pope   M. K. Pope, *From Latin to Modern French* (Manchester, 1934; rev. ed. 1952).

R.E.W.   W. Meyer-Lübke, *Romanisches Etymologisches Wörterbuch* (3rd ed., Heidelberg, 1935).

S.A.T.F.   Société des Anciens Textes Français.

T.-L.   A. Tobler and E. Lommatzsch, *Altfranzösisches Wörterbuch* (Berlin-Wiesbaden, 1925–).

INTRODUCTION

TITLE

THE title, *Le Petit Plet*, which has been used since de la Rue's indication of the work, is found in the *incipit* of the poem in the three manuscripts *LOV* (for these sigla, see below), in the *explicit* of *V*, as well as in line 11 of the text.

THE MANUSCRIPTS

There are three extant copies of the *Petit Plet*.

L London, British Museum, Cotton Caligula A 9. This is a parchment manuscript, probably of the first half of the thirteenth century, containing French and English works. It has 261 folios according to its modern foliation, measures 210 by 150 mm., and is bound in leather. The *Petit Plet* has two columns to the page, averaging 35 lines a column, 1780 lines in all.

Contents:

1. fol. 3r—a version of Layamon's *Brut*.[1] The first folio has fine red and blue illuminations; the first majuscule depicts a clerical scribe at work. Fol. 3r bears the signature 'Robertus Cotton Bruce'.

2. fol. 195r—*La Vie de seint Josaphaz*, an Anglo-Norman poem by Chardri.[2]

3. fol. 216v—*Les Set Dormanz*, an Anglo-Norman poem by Chardri.[2]

4. fol. 229v—an Anglo-Norman chronicle of the Anglo-Saxon and Norman kings of England up to the death of John.[3]

5. fol. 233r—one of the two extant copies of the *Owl and the Nightingale*.[4] The second is in Oxford, Jesus College 29 (our MS. *O*).

6. fol. 246r—a group of seven short Middle English poems, all

---

[1] Ed. Sir Frederick Madden (London, 1847); G. L. Brook and R. F. Leslie, E.E.T.S. 250, vol. 1 (Oxford, 1963).
[2] Ed. Koch, op. cit.
[3] Ed. Christian Foltys (Inaugural-Dissertation, Berlin, 1962, offset).
[4] Several editions: see especially J. E. Wells (Boston and London, 1907); J. W. H. Atkins (Cambridge, 1922); J. H. G. Grattan, E.E.T.S. Extra Series 119 (Oxford, 1935); E. G. Stanley (London, 1960). The manuscripts are reproduced in facsimile by N. R. Ker, E.E.T.S. 251 (London and New York, 1963).

published by Richard Morris in *An Old English Miscellany*[1] under the following titles: *Long Life*, *An Orison of Our Lady*, *Will and Wit*, *Doomsday*, *Death*, *Ten Abuses*, *A lutel soth Sermon*. Carleton Brown includes *Doomsday* (*Latemest Day*) and *Will and Wit* in his *English Lyrics of the Thirteenth Century*.[2] All except *Will and Wit* appear also in our MS. *O*.

7. fol. 249r—the *Petit Plet*. *Josaphaz*, the *Set Dormanz* and the *Petit Plet* appear to have been written by the same scribe, as lay-out and hand seem identical in all three. The *Petit Plet* is introduced by the *incipit*: 'Ici com̄ce le petit plet.' Each section of the poem begins with a large red initial and the initial letter of each line is daubed with red; occasionally letters within the line are similarly marked, e.g. the *s* of *fust* (l. 66), *ester* (l. 249). The two participants in the debate are usually introduced on each occasion by the words *l'enfant* or *le veillard*, often abbreviated, written in red in the right-hand margin, generally beside the last line spoken by the adversary. These indications are missing at ll. 312, 314, 318, 320, 364, 366, 598, 599, etc. The manuscript is clear and legible except for parts of fol. 216r (ll. 1710, 1727–9) and the verso of the same folio where the writing has been almost effaced by rubbing against the cover. For a discussion of the manuscript's dating, see below, p. xxxi.

O Oxford, Jesus College 29. This manuscript, which has been on permanent loan to the Bodleian Library since 1886, is in two parts, the first of paper and vellum, the second of vellum, totalling 257 folios. It measures 181 by 133 mm. and is leather-bound. The *Petit Plet* has two columns to a page, an average of 32 lines a column, 1649 lines in all, the lacuna being caused by a missing folio between foll. 247 and 248. The two parts are from once separate manuscripts. The first part of 143 folios contains only an incomplete Latin chronicle, the second of 114 folios an anthology of English and French pieces, several of which appear also in *L*.

Contents:

1. Part I, fol. 1r—a fifteenth-century Latin chronicle of the kings of England from 900 to 1445.

2. Part II, fol. 144r—*The Passion of Our Lord*, a Middle English poem.[3]

---

[1] E.E.T.S. 49 (London, 1872).
[2] Oxford, 1932.
[3] Morris, op. cit., pp. 37–57.

3. fol. 156r—*The Owl and the Nightingale*, the second of the two extant copies.[1]

4. fol. 169r—the *Poema Morale*.[2]

5. fol. 175r—a group of Middle English poems of varying length, including the *Proverbs of Alfred*.[3] Within the group is one prose piece, the *Shires and Hundreds of England*.[4]

6. fol. 195v—a fragment of 315 lines of the *Vie de Tobie*, an Anglo-Norman poem by 'Guillaume le Clerc' of Normandy.[5]

7. fol. 198r—*The Eleven Pains of Hell*, a Middle English poem introduced by six lines of French.[6]

8. fol. 201r—the *Doctrinal*, in Anglo-Norman.[7]

9. fol. 207v—*La Vie de set Dormaunz*, by Chardri.

10. fol. 233r—*La Vie seynt Josaphaz*, by Chardri.

11. fol. 244v—the *Petit Plet*. Because of the missing leaf between foll. 247–8, ll. 440–567 are wanting. In addition, ll. 228–9 and ll. 1770–1 have been telescoped, while an extra line, a repetition of l. 339, is found between ll. 378–9. The large coloured capitals are in red and blue, though not regularly alternated as was presumably intended. The sections are introduced by the words *Le Juvencel* or *Le Veyllard*, placed in the centre of the column, but not always indicating the correct speaker. The errors have been emended by a later hand. Possibly a second scribe was responsible for the headings and coloured initials. The main scribe is much less reliable than the scribe of *L*.

Much has been written by scholars about this manuscript (and its famous 'broken leaf') which need not be repeated here.[8] A most

---

[1] Cf. p. xi, n. 4.

[2] Morris, op. cit., pp. 58–71.

[3] All except the last, *Assisa panis Angliae* (fol. 195r) are included in Morris, op. cit., pp. 72–130, 141–4, 156–91. Five appear in Carleton Brown, op. cit., pp. 19, 65, 67, 68. A detailed description is found in Ker, op. cit., pp. ix–x. For the *Proverbs of Alfred*, see the edition by O. S. Anderson Arngart, Skrifter Utgivana av Kungl. Humanistiska Vetenskapssamfundet i Lund XXXII (Lund, vol. I, 1942, vol. II, 1955).

[4] Morris, op. cit., pp. 145–6.

[5] Ed. Robert Reinsch, *Archiv für das Studium der Neueren Sprachen u. Literaturen* 62 (1879), 375–96.

[6] Morris, op. cit., pp. 147–55.

[7] This is one of 26 copies of the *Doctrinal Sauvage* (see P. Meyer, *Romania* 6 (1877), 20–2, 16 (1887), 60–1). The version in MS. Paris BN 837, which differs considerably from the above, was published by A. Jubinal, *Nouveau recueil de contes . . .* (Paris, 1839–42) 2, 150–61. The *Doctrinal* has been re-edited by A. Sakari, Studia Philologica Jyvaskylaensia III (Jyvaskyla, 1967).

[8] Grattan, op. cit., pp. xv–xviii; Wells, op. cit., pp. vii–xvii; C. L. Wrenn, 'Curiosities in a medieval manuscript', *Essays and Studies* XXV (1939), 101–15.

complete and up-to-date study of its dating and history has been made by Dr. Betty Hill.[1] Miss Hill shows that the date of Part II, previously considered from internal evidence of the *Vie de Tobie* to be 1276–9,[2] can no longer be placed so precisely, and concludes from an examination of the preceding piece, *Assisa panis Angliae*, that it can only be dated *post* 1256. In addition, Miss Hill gives an interesting account of how the manuscript could have come into the possession of the Rev. Thomas Wilkins whose signature appears on the fly-leaf and who donated the manuscript to Jesus College, Oxford.[3]

The relation between *L* and *O* has aroused considerable scholarly interest, as they contain so many pieces in common.[4] A study of the filiation of the *Petit Plet* corroborates the assertion that *O* is not a copy of *L*, but that the scribe of *O* must have had before him a manuscript containing the same pieces as *L*, probably in the same order.

V Vatican, MS. Reg. lat. 1659. This parchment manuscript is also composed of two distinct and originally separate parts. It measures 257 by 149 mm.; the *Petit Plet* has two columns to a page, averaging 62 lines a column.

Contents:

1. Part I, fol. 1r—*L'Estoire de la Guerre Sainte* of Ambroise.[5]

2. fol. 89v—two stanzas of the *planh* by Gaucelm Faidit on the death of Richard I,[6] with musical notes.

3. Part II, fol. 91r—the *Petit Plet*.

4. fol. 98r, col. 2—a number of proverbs about women.

5. fol. 98v—a fragment of 414 lines of the *Petite Philosophie*.[7]

Part II is written in a fourteenth-century hand.[8] The scribe of the *Petit Plet* seems to have intended beginning some sections with a large or coloured initial, as spaces are left for them in some lines (1, 21, 97, 615). However, he appears to have changed his mind and simply indicates the sections with two strokes beside the initial letter

---

[1] 'The History of Jesus College, Oxford MS. 29', *Medium Aevum* XXXII, No. 3 (1963), 203–13.

[2] Anna Paues, 'A newly discovered manuscript of the *Poema Morale*', *Anglia* 30 (1907), 222.

[3] For a discussion of the donation, see Wrenn, op. cit., pp. 102–4, 113–14, and Miss Hill, p. 206, n. 16.

[4] See Ker, op. cit., pp. ix–xi.

[5] Ed. Gaston Paris, *Coll. Doc. inéd.* I, 11 (Paris, 1897).

[6] R. T. Hill and T. G. Bergin, *Anthology of the Provençal Troubadours*, Yale Romanic Studies XVII (New Haven, 1941), 144–6; Jean Mouzat, *Les poèmes de Gaucelm Faidit* (Paris, 1965), pp. 415–18.

[7] Ed. Trethewey, op. cit.

[8] Prof. Trethewey gives a detailed description of the manuscript, pp. xiii–xiv.

or by a capital slightly larger than normal. A couplet has been inserted between ll. 378–9 (the first line of which, as in *O*, repeats l. 339), but l. 364 is missing. A line rhyming with l. 363 has been written in the right-hand margin by a later hand. There are other markings present too: marginal comments are found beside ll. 1217, 1375; ll. 1413–14 are repeated at the foot of fol. 96r, col. 2. Perhaps this same 'scribbler' is responsible for the hands and faces drawn on foll. 92v, 95v, 96r. The scribe of *V* is also less reliable than the scribe of *L*.

The history of *V*, once the property of Queen Christina of Sweden, is traced by G. Paris in his introduction to the *Estoire*.[1] As mentioned above, in the Preface, Adelbert Keller published the first 366 lines of the *Petit Plet* and the last 13 lines of the *Petite Philosophie* (ll. 569–81 in Prof. Trethewey's edition), believing them to be part of the same poem. This repeats an error of the Vatican catalogue, an eighteenth-century inventory, which under Article 1659 lists the contents as 'Romanicum Gallicum de bello sacro—Qui longue Aliud eadem lingua inscriptum 1. le Periplee'.[2]

Of the three manuscripts, *L* is the oldest, the most complete and the most reliable, having fewer individual faults than *O* or *V*, and is thus the obvious choice as the base manuscript for the text.

Abbreviations and Accents

Abbreviations and contractions are frequent in all three manuscripts. In resolving each case I have referred where possible to the most frequently occurring orthographical form in each manuscript, as in many instances the scribes present more than one complete spelling. Where no complete orthographical form exists, the word has been resolved analogically or arbitrarily. Only the cases where variation is possible are listed. The sign > in the three paragraphs below represents 'is (are) transcribed as'.

L *ml't* 15, etc. > *mult* 9, etc. (7 examples); *mut* is found once 75. 9 before *m* > *com*: *9munement* 503 (*cōmune* 572); before other consonants > *cun*: *9fort* 378, etc. (*cunfort* 320, etc.). *p* > *par*: *p* 40, etc. (*par* 23, etc.) or *per*: *pdu* 151 (*perdi* 1061); the expansion of *apnent* 34 to *apernent* is arbitrary. *p* > *pro*: *peme* 40 (*proeme* 826) or > *pru*:

[1] Pp. i–vi.
[2] E. Langlois, *Notices et Extraits des Manuscrits* XXXIII, 2e partie (Paris, 1889), 192–3, also repeated the error, even though Koch's edition had appeared in 1879.

B

pedom 90, etc. (*prudum* 882, etc., 3 examples, *produme* 782). ˜ above
a letter > *ur*: *avent˜es* 273, etc. (*aventure* 23, etc.), *c˜age* 528, 1417
(*curage* 13, etc., 7 examples, *corage* 411), *hon˜* 1504 by analogy with
amur 1344, etc.; *m˜nes* 83, etc. is arbitrary; and > *or*: *p˜* 24, etc.
(*por* 1, etc.), the future forms of *poeir* 122, 144, 148, etc. (*porra*, etc.
621, 829, etc.); the future forms of *morir* are resolved by analogy with
the forms of *poeir*, as is *dem˜ra* 262. In one case *p˜* 1596 > *par*. The
vertical zigzag above a letter > *er*: *s⁴reit* 150, etc. (*serreit* 231, etc.);
or > *re*: *p⁴ndreit* 1448 (*prendre*[ʒ] 283). Vowels written above the
line > *r* + vowel: *est⁰nge* 108, etc., or > *u* + vowel: *nasqⁱstes* 315; *mᶜci*
239 > *merci*. The straight bar above a letter indicates *n* or *m*; in
com̄ce incipit and *am̄* 1779, 1780 it is resolved *en*. *Dſ* 940 > *Deus*; *ē*
123, etc. > *est*; *ūre* 106, etc. > *vostre*. The sign ⁚ 975 > *est*.

   O   9 before *m* > *cum* (*cum̄encez* 287); elsewhere > *con* (*confort* 342,
etc.). *p* > *par* or *per* (see examples for L). *p* > *pro*: *pmesse* 1622,
pmettreyent 1635. ˜ above a letter is always *ur*. The zigzag above a
letter > *er*: *av⁴* 24, etc. Vowels written above the line are expanded
as in L. *m⁰rtyre* 776 is of course not an abbreviation. The nasal bar,
in addition to representing *n* or *m*, can be read as vowel + *n*: *ſt* 695,
etc., *bonem̄t* 795, *m̄d* 384, *am̄* 1779, 1780. *k̷* is interpreted as *kar* 15, 19,
etc., *ke* 343, *ki* 384.

   V   *mlt*, *ml't* > *mut* which is found in all complete readings except
for *mult* 264. 9 before *m* > *com*, elsewhere *con*. *p* > *par* or *per* (see
examples for L). *p* > *pro*: *espeue* 733 (*esproue* 736) or > *pru*: *pdom* 90,
etc., by analogy with *pru* 204, etc. ⁴ above a letter > *er* or *re*, but in
two cases I have transcribed it as *ro*: *p⁴mettre* 170, *p⁴mettrunt* 1635.
Vowels above the line and the nasal bar are transcribed as in L and O.
Only *q̄* 12, etc. > *que*, *conq̄rez* 404 > *conquerez* are peculiar to *V*.
k̷ 19, etc. > *kar*; *k̷k̷e* 567 > *keke*.

   The only accent that appears is a diagonal stroke over *i* (*LOV*)
when there is a possibility of confusion, while O occasionally has
the stroke over *e*, without, however, any consistency in its use.

Manuscript Filiation

   As already stated, MS. O is not a copy of L but, as examination
shows, forms a group with *V* against L. *OV* share ten evident errors
not found in L: ll. 1379–80 are interverted in *OV*, while L retains the
logical order; ll. 345, 375, 695, 1013, 1029, 1259, 1379, 1431, 1455,
1720 have errors common only to *OV*. Other possible errors are also

found to substantiate the grouping OV against L. The absence of the article before *liu* in l. 75 appears incorrect. The reading *A ces* in OV 159 instead of *Assez* L could be a fault or an orthographic variant. *Deverez* OV 798 is not the tense expected after *mesdeist* 796, but again this is a weak case, considering the confusion of tense sequence in continental and insular French.[1] The singular form of the article before plural noun and adjective in OV 1487 appears to be an error, although a weak basis for classification.

Neither of the other possible groupings, LV against O, LO against V, provides as substantial a list of common faults, although there are examples in the latter grouping where V has the better reading: V 260 is obviously correct, but the opposition *sai/sui* is weak; V 712 is more comprehensible than 'Ki primes l'ad gueres ne munte' of LO, but one is inclined to impute 'E puis i verrez quei amounte' in V to the scribe who may also have found the line difficult. V may also be preferable in ll. 50 and 200. V 909 *dirrez* is correct but O is wanting here. The only positive example where O is better than LV is *peot* O 1526 instead of *poez*, while *a mal* O 1450 is certainly the more common expression. From these comparisons, then, it is evident that OV form a solid group against L.

A further problem arises, however, when one notes probable errors common to all three manuscripts, which suggest the existence of a faulty copy (X) prior to LOV but later than the original. The occurrence of *se tint* 479 is such a case and other examples providing similar evidence are *mult vaut* 581, *ne larrad* 921, *Ki les cerchast* 1334, *e Deus i mist* 1751, also the probable interversion of ll. 49–50 (see the notes on these lines). The manuscript stemma would then be:

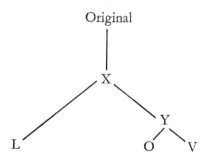

Original

X

Y

L   O   V

[1] Brunot I, 255; see examples in R.-L. Wagner, *Les Phrases hypothétiques commençant par 'si'* . . . (Paris, 1939), p. 469.

LANGUAGE

A. *Phonology*

The *Petit Plet* gives evidence of a number of phonological changes which have been rare in twelfth-century texts but which will appear with greater frequency during the thirteenth century. The following is a list of the more important features apparent in the rhymes.

1. ę (< tonic checked ĭ, ē) rhymes with e (< tonic checked ĕ, or ai) in *vaslet* 107 (: *ret*), 287 (: *plet*), *ele* 1191 (: *gravele*). This is one of the first occurrences of the rhyme other than before l or a consonantal group.[1]

2. The diphthong ei in infinitive endings rhymes with e (< tonic free a), *arder* 668 (: *esgarder*), *aver* 964 (: *aver* < *avarum*), 988 (: *amer* < *amarum*), 991 (: *penser*), and also with e reduced from ie, *saver* 682 (: *reprover*), *aver* 1736 (: *leger*). In the rhyme *crere* : *terre* 843, ei reduces to rhyme with e (< tonic checked ĕ).[2]

3. ei and ai are found together in several rhymes: (a) before a final consonant, *treis* 787 (: *mauveis*), *reis* 1119 (: *paleis*), *seit* 1428, 1591 (: *eit*), *treis* 1630 (: *verrais*); (b) final in syllable, *curteise* 1215 (: *mauveise*), *eire* 1296 (: *deboneire*); (c) final in word, *quai* 44 (: *ai*), *quei* 911 (: *dirrai*). In (a) and (b) it is probable that the phonetic value of both diphthongs is ę; ai : ę is found frequently, though only one example of ei : ę is present, 843. In final position the value appears uncertain.[3]

4. Before feminine ę, ei (graphy *oi*) rhymes with oi < au + yod, *voie* 228, 996, 1197 (: *joie*), *proie* 1471 (: *joie*).

5. ie from any source is reduced to e, rhyming freely with e < tonic free a, *enginner* 40 (: *penser*), *verger* 46 (: *penser*), *arere* 673, 836, 1211, 1386 (: *pere*), *fevre* 757 (: *levre*), *manere* 762 (: *frere*), *mester* 1618 (: *amer*), etc. This e (< ie) also rhymes with e (< ei) in infinitive endings (see above).

6. ai (< a + yod) reduces to e and is found in rhyme with e (< tonic checked ĕ), *mestre* 121, etc. (: *estre*), *affere* 403, etc. (: *terre*). ai of Germanic origin is found only in rhymes with ai (< a + yod), the graphy being, however, *e*.

---

[1] J. Vising, 'Die E-Laute im Reime der anglonormannischen Dichter des XII. Jahrhunderts', *Zeitschrift für französische Sprache u. Literatur* 39 (1912), 7; Pope § 1145.

[2] Cf. John E. Matzke, ed. *Les Œuvres de Simund de Freine*, S.A.T.F. 75 (1909), *Rom. de Phil.* l. 518, *St. Georges* l. 584.

[3] For a discussion of ei:ai rhymes, see J. Vising, *Etude sur le dialecte anglo-normand du XIIe siècle* (Upsala, 1882), p. 75; Trethewey, op. cit., pp. xxix–xxxi, pp. xlviii–l.

7. The usual Anglo-Norman distinction between **an** and **en** is maintained, although *dolent* rhymes both in **an** 590 and **en** 83, 1082.[1]

8. **ain** does not rhyme with **ein** in spite of frequent orthographical confusion. The absence of distinction between these two sounds is noted as early as the *Brendan*.[2]

9. **ǫ** free rhymes with **ǫ** checked, both written *u*, *dolur* 47, 219 (: *sujur*), *tristur* 257 (: *sujur*), *vus* 269 (: *curuʒ*), *pruʒ* 537, etc. (: *tuʒ*), etc.

10. Only once is there a possible rhyme **u** (< tonic free **ǫ**) : **ü** (< **ū**), *pour* 1068 (: *seur*). *Pour* also rhymes with *jur* 1670, but *pavor* gave doublet forms[3] and authors were known to use both.[4]

11. **üi** (< **ǒ** + yod and **ū** + yod) reduces to **ü** and rhymes with **ü** (< **ū**), *puis* 297 (: *cunfus*), *dedure* 1 (: *esveisure*), *su* 1438 (: *fu* 3rd person).

12. **üi** (< **ū** + yod) preceded by **k** became an ascending diphthong in Anglo-Norman, **ẅi**, and rhymes with **i**, *quit* 286 (: *mesdit*).

13. **locum** > **liu**, *liu* 75 (: *fiu* < *feudum*); *fiu* appears to be a reduction of *fieu*, a Picard influence.[5]

14. Weak **ę** presumably falls in *redutee* (masc.) 755 (: *espee*) and in both *munde* 1085 and *amunte* 1086 (see note on l. 1085).

15. No confusion is made between **l** and **λ**. Preconsonantal **l** preceded by **i** has disappeared, *fiʒ* 161, etc. (: *diʒ*), *gentiʒ* 517 (: *pais*); preceded by **u**, it merges with the vowel, *mult* 739 (: *tut*), *escut* 815 (: *tut*), etc.; after **a** and **e** vocalization is suggested by the orthography, *haut* 65, etc., *chaut* 66, etc., *Meuʒ* 194, etc., *leaus* 1582, 1616, etc.

16. There is no distinction in rhyme between **r** and **rr**, *affere* 403, etc. (: *terre*), *crere* 843 (: *terre*), etc. **r** has fallen before **s**, *plusurs* 580 (: *dolerus*).

17. Final **m** and **n** are not distinguished, *renun* (< *nōmen*) 789 (: *nun* < *nōn*), *feim* 905 (: *demein*), etc. Neither is **m** distinguished from **mm**, *pome* 781 (: *produme*), etc. Final **n** falls after **r**, *sujur* 48, etc. (: *dolur*).

18. *f* is sometimes written before final **s**, but rhymes indicate that it is mute, *mendifs* 1124 (: *fiʒ*), etc.

19. Preconsonantal **s** falls, *tantost* 560 (: *mot*), *abisme* 1601 (: *fausime*),

---

[1] P. Meyer, 'Phonétique française: AN et EN toniques', *Mémoires de la Société de Linguistique de Paris* I, 263 (Paris, 1870).
[2] Ed. E. G. R. Waters (Oxford, 1928), p. cxl, feminine rhymes only.
[3] F.E.W. 8, 90, n. 21.
[4] *Le Jeu de S. Nicolas* of Jean Bodel (ed. F. J. Warne, Oxford, 1951) has *peür* 572: *asseur* 569 and *paour* 550: *Sauveour* 551; cf. *Set Dormanz*, *pour* 1610: *aseur* and *pour* 160: *creatur*, etc.
[5] Pope § 1168 and p. 488, § vi.

nasqui(s)tes 315, 455 (: *quites*), etc., but it would appear to be retained in *test* (pres. ind.3) 1302 (: *est*, noun) and *fist* (pret.3) 913 (*porveist*, imp. subj.3).[1]

20. **z** < **t** or **d** + **s**, λ + **s**, **k** + yod rhymes with **s**, *pruz* 575 (: *vigerus*), *lebarz* 640 (: *ars*), *gentiz* 517 (: *pais*), *solas* 120 (: *pas*).

For **t** in verbal endings, see below, Morphology.

B. *Morphology*

1. *Declension*. In spite of frequent confusion in the use of cases, there is a tendency towards generalization of the oblique case, particularly among nouns. In the nominative singular of masculine parisyllabic nouns, the flexional -*s*/-*z* occurs in rhyme only in *fiz* 161, 338, etc. (: *diz*, obl. pl.), and *letanz* 173 (: *anz*, obl. pl.); the -*s* is also implied in *cheitif* nom. sg. 1505 (: *pris*). Within the line[2] are *reis* 80, 1135, *Deus* 940, etc., and further examples of *fiz* 319, etc. With masculine adjectives of the same type, retention of -*s*/-*z* is more frequent in rhyme, a ratio of approximately 1 : 5, *senez* 102 (: *demenez*), *lez* 158 (: *esmerveillez*), *quites* 316, 456 (: *nasqui(s)tes*), *gentiz* 517 (: *pais*), etc. It is rare to find an -*s*/-*z* form in parisyllabic nouns or adjectives functioning as an oblique, *reis* 1119 (: *paleis*), *fiz* 1123 (: *mendifs*), *leaus* 1582 (: *maus*). The nominative plural of this type shows three nouns out of five with -*s*/-*z*, *wandelarz* 979 (: *parz*, obl. pl.), *dez* 1370 (: *mentez*), *enemis* 1589 (: *dis* < *decem*); cf. *veisin* 866 (: *fin*), *chevaler* 1268 (: *esmerveiller*). Within the line only *arbre* 65 has no -*s*. For *covenant* 1298, see note on this line. Nominative plural adjectives have -*s*/-*z* in only two cases out of seven, *tuz* (pron.) 569 (: *desuz*), *verrais* 1629 (: *treis*), excluding an interrhyme, but graphically the -*s* is elsewhere dominant.

Parisyllabic nouns and adjectives of the type *pere/povre* do not take an analogical -*s* in rhyme, though we find *povres* 983 within the line, a purely orthographical example.

Confusion in masculine imparisyllabics is exemplified by the occurrence in the nominative of *larun* 817 and *lere* 1398, *hoem* 178, etc. and *home* 720 (: *summe*), etc., *prudum* 882 (: *resun*), etc. and *prudume* 1535 (: *Rume*). The appearance of the last two pairs in oblique positions as well would indicate that forms were used to suit metre and rhyme rather than case function. In the plural both nominative

---

[1] F. J. Tanquerey, *L'Evolution du verbe en anglo-français* (*XIIe–XIVe siècles*) (Paris, 1915), p. 119.
[2] Unless otherwise specified, all references within the line are to the base manuscript *L*.

and oblique cases have forms with and without -*s*. For a discussion of *leres* 37, see Notes.

Parisyllabic feminine nouns and adjectives of the type *mere/bone* are regular except for *nul*, etc., before vowels. Parisyllabics of the type *flur/vertu* have no -*s* in the nom. sg., *gent* 831 (: *apertement*), *flur* 1759 (: *entur*), etc. Feminine imparisyllabics show the oblique form for the nominative function, *greinnur* 1179, etc.

Analogical -*e* in feminine adjectives of the Latin third declension is found frequently, *forte* 747, *mortele* 393, etc., but the only cases in rhyme are those known to have had distinct feminine forms much earlier than most adjectives, *sutive* 61 (: *vive*), *commune* 572 (: *Fortune*), *fine* 945 (: *enterrine*), *curteise* 1215 (: *maveise*); there is one interrhyme, *leale* 1387 : *cursale*. *Grant* remains unchanged, 79 (: *tant*), etc.

Neuter adjective forms in rhyme are regular, but within the line an analogical -*s* occasionally appears, *veirs* 123, etc.

In the past participle masc. sg. nom., forms without -*s*/-*z* predominate; in the masc. pl. nom., forms having -*s*/-*z* are more frequent, though these are within the line.

All manuscripts present *li* and *le* in the masc. sg. nom. of the definite article, the proportions being 1:1 in *L*, 3:5 in *O*, 5:3 in *V*. Only in *V* does *li* appear as an oblique, 1032. In the masc. pl. nom. *li* is less frequent than *les*, 1:4 in *L*, 1:2 in *OV*. The scribe of *V* often writes *le* for *les* before consonants.[1] In *L le* also occurs before some feminine nouns beginning with a vowel or mute *h*,[2] 870, 1613, etc., and also before *verdur* 71 which may be a mistake of gender (cf. *la pire OV* 1604 and *la penser V* 669). Note also *la robes rutes OV* 1487. The usual contractions of preposition and article are common, sometimes reduced in *OV* to *a, de*, but note *De le men cors* 656.

In the indefinite article the -*s* has disappeared from the masc. sg. nom. and the only unusual form is *unt V* 688 before *tel*, surely an error. Several times *e* of *une* is elided before a vowel, 2, 521, etc. Before *langur* 1038, *un* perhaps indicates a gender confusion. Numeral adjectives are regular except for *unes V* 295 (sg. obl.) and *unz V* 1665 (sg. obl.).

Jo and *jeo* are used without distinction as tonic and atonic forms of the first person pronoun, *jeo* appearing in the only rhyme, 439 (: *volunté*). *O* uses *jeo* only, *V jo* and *joe*. *Mei* and *me* are confused in the atonic position by the scribes of *L* and *V*, as are *tei* and *te*. *L* has *li* for *le*, atonic acc. sg., 277, 482, 484 (see Notes to ll. 277, 482). The tonic accusative forms of the third person sg. masc. and fem. are both *li*, occurring in rhyme with *i*, masc. 1411, 1620, fem. 1201, 1398.

Confusion of the relative pronouns *ki*, *ke* is common in the nominative, but *ki* rarely appears as an oblique, 32, 1760.

Among demonstratives *cil* in the masc. sg. nom., 87, 121, etc., is dominant over *celui* 174, 1124, etc., while in the oblique case *celui* is the usual form, except for *cel* 92 and *icel L* 93 (doubtful, see note) which are both adjectival. (*I*)*ceus* predominates over *cil* in the masc. pl. nom.

In *L* 1437, *celu* is probably a scribal error. The old neuter survives in *poet cel estre* 414, etc. Of *cist* forms the most frequent graphy is (*i*)*cest* 12, 56, etc., with *cist* occurring only twice, 722, 1029. The neuter is (*i*)*ceo*, once *c'* 1553. In the fem. pl. obl. the spelling *ses* 864 should be noted.

Oblique forms have been generalized among possessive pronouns, except for *mi* 866, a masc. pl. nom. Only *mun L* 127 (*O men*) is found before a feminine noun beginning with a vowel; elsewhere *ma*, *ta*, *sa* are in use.[1]

One may note the following variety of forms for *l'on*: *l'un*, *un*, *l'en*, *l'em* as well as *hoem*, *hume*, *home*.

2. *Conjugation.* There are six examples in rhyme of the passage of infinitives in *-eir* to *-er*, *arder* 668 (: *esgarder*), *saver* 682 (: *repruver*), *aver* 964 (: *aver < avarum*), 988 (: *amer < amarum*), 991 (: *penser*), 1736 (: *leger*). Forms in *-eir* remain, 1046, 1136, 1598, etc. The MS. *V* spellings *pensir* 45, 477, *hastir* 149, *do(i)lir* 190, 322, etc., are purely scribal in origin.[2] The reduction of the diphthong *ie* to *e* (see Phonology) is also evident in infinitives in *-ier*, as well as other verbal endings containing *ie*.

First person sg. pres. ind. forms of the first conjugation do not take an analogical *e*, *pens* 105 (: *sens*), *chant* 553 (: *enfant*), etc. *V* does present *merveylle* 431, possibly supported by the syllabic count. First person sg. analogical *s* in third conjugation verbs does not appear in rhyme, *di* 365 (: *marri*), etc. Similarly the final palatal in *teng* 169, etc., which is presumably phonetic, occurs only graphically. Also to be noted is the scribal vocalization of *l* in *apeau* 439.

---

[1] P. Rickard, *Archivum Linguisticum* 11 (1959), 21–47, 115–47.
[2] *V* commonly employs the graphy *i* for *e*, *chif* 1451, *chir* 1607, etc.

Elision and retention of final *-e* <-at before a vowel are equally frequent, both in indicative and subjunctive third person forms, 543, 603, etc., 154, 235, etc.

The fall of *-e*, ind. pr.3 first conjugation ending, is likely in *amunte* 1086 (see note on l. 1085). Final supported *t* in the third person sg. pres. ind. third conjugation remains, *mesdit* 285 (: *quit*), while other third person dentals occurring graphically are *ad* 120, etc., *amat* (pret.) 901, *frat* 393, *serrat* 508, *serrad* 776, *larrad* 921.

Aler shows only the form *vet* in the third person sg., 49, etc.

The only rhymed case of the first person plural is *-uns*, *lerruns* 1430 (: *acheisuns*), but orthographically *-um* is commoner, *avum* 572, etc.

Generally the second person plural ending is *-ez*, for which MS. *L* provides three interesting scribal variants: *-et*,[1] *bainet* 103, *usset* 594, *seet* 1237; *-er*, *vuler* 342, *morrer* 364, *sacher* 1431; *-és*, *venkés* 745.

The weak *e* of endings *-eie*, *-eient* seems for the most part to drop, though versificational irregularities prevent a precise conclusion. Confusion of future and conditional forms arises when scribes drop the *e*, *saverei L* 451.

The imprecise nature of the versification also confuses discussion of diaeresis and synaeresis. In verb forms with *ei*, the *ei* apparently represents one syllable in all cases, *feistes* 114, *preisse* 142, *feist* 301, etc., while forms in *eu* appear to be disyllabic in about 25 per cent of cases, *seust* 182, 1186 (both doubtful), *eust* 270, 1350, etc.

Confusion exists in the base manuscript *L* between first and third person sg. future endings, *girra* 623 = *girrai*, *frai* 1366 = *fra*. The usual O.F. contractions in the future of *-ner-*, *-rer-*, are found in *endurra* 104, *dorra* (= *donnera*) 191, 1508, *demorra* 262, etc. The future radical of *fere* is reduced to *fr-*, though *freez* 281 might be considered an example of metathesis.[2] *Recuverai* 1083 could be the result of metathesis, followed by reduction of the double *r* so formed, or more simply the result of dissimilation of *recuvrerai*. Non-etymological doubling of *r* occurs in *dirrai*, etc., 336, etc., *girra* 623, etc. The etymological future of *estre* is found only in the third person sg., *ert* 444, 538, etc., slightly more common than *serra*, etc. 316, 346, etc. Svarabhaktic *e* is found in futures and conditionals of third conjugation verbs, but as with etymological *e* of first conjugation futures

---

[1] Pope § 1295 (i).
[2] Tanquerey, op. cit., p. 212, sees it as a doubling of the vowel. A syllabic count of the line, however, makes the word monosyllabic.

and conditionals, it has lost its syllabic value in most cases, *averei* 151, 1606, *avera* 239, etc., as it has in the infinitives, *coverir* 894, *descoverir* 954, *recoverer* 1423, *vivere* 1523 (: *delivre*). *Vivere* 129 is less certain. In most instances the scribes seem to have used the *e* simply to indicate the consonantal value of *u*.

In first conjugation verbs, the western termination of the imperfect indicative *-out* appears four times in the spellings in all MSS. (once *-ot V* 1241), *esbaneout* 23, *rouleout* 60, *resemblout* 62, 1241, but elsewhere endings of the second and third conjugations are used. Both third person sg. forms of *estre* are employed, *esteit* 21, 58, etc., *ert* 570, 1470; *esteit* 1183 (: *dreit*) is the only rhymed example.

Among the weak preterites *morirent* 354 (: *furent*) is purely graphic. Of the strong preterites, *fere* shows *fiz* 1718 (: *fiz* < *filius*) and *firent* 673, 1394; *tut* 1087 (< *tacuit*, Pope § 1020, Type A) rhymes with *mut* (Pope ibid., Type C). The diphthong of Type A appears within the line in *out* 79, 80, etc. In the first person sg. of the preterite, *estre* gives both *fu* and *fui*, neither in rhyme, 132, 870, 1335.

Several verbs have present subjunctives in *-ge*, though without conclusive rhymes, *moergez* 349, 443, *tenge* 819, *devenge* 1355, etc. *Dechece* 605 is a Northern form, common also in Anglo-Norman.[1] Third person sg. forms remain without *-e* in the first conjugation, *gart/d* 98, 384, etc., except *guie* 400 whose radical ends in a vowel.[2] *Duner* gives *doint* 42, 54, etc.; *V* uses *doyne* 226, etc., and *doinst* 1775 as well. *Plaire* retains the third person sg. pres. subj. form *place* in the formula *ne place a Deu* 882, 918, but elsewhere has *pleise* 523, 567(: *eise*).

O provides a rare imperfect subjunctive form *ussessez* 878; *deytes O* 1315 (variant of *deistes L*) is most likely a perfect; *meitent V* 490 (variant of *meissent L*) is perhaps present indicative.

The past participle of *remaneir* is *remis* 646. One may also note *vesqui* (*nasquy O*) 1588 (: *ami*), *irascu* 625 (: *nu*), and *cheet* 860 (for *cheeit*, *cheoit*, Pope § 1051).

C. *Syntax*

The definite article is lacking before *mor* 1114 and *jur* 1649.

As already noted there is some confusion of gender; *amur* 32, 1650 and perhaps *langur* 737, 763, 1038 (cf. p. xxi) show both genders. *Creature* 929 is qualified by masculine adjectives *beauz*, *runz* 930,

---

[1] Pope § 1276.   [2] Pope § 909.

dolurs 601 by *tanz*, though *OV tauntes* is preferable here for metrical reasons, *acheisuns* 1429 by *muz*, and *aventures* 693 by *tanz* (but this is probably for *tant* adverbial).

The oblique case is occasionally used as a possessive, 186, 371, 511, 1536, where the possessor is a person. This function is once indicated by *a*, 1400.

In his use of personal pronouns, the author changes indifferently from *tu* to *vus*, *vus* often being followed by *tun*, etc., 166, 180, 278, etc. The relative *ki* sometimes represents *celui qui*, 237, 327, etc.; *ke* 1422 = *ce qui*; *ke* 1327, 1402 = *ce que*. Except for the feminines, *cil* forms of the demonstrative are generally pronominal. In *OV il* is often a variant of *cil*, *O* 121, 289, etc., *V* 255, 289, etc. *Cist* forms are usually adjectival, though once *cest* functions as a pronoun, 1106. Conversely *V* uses *ço/ceo* as an adjective, 302, 886, 1085. The tonic possessive pronoun preceded by the article is employed as an adjective, *la nostre vie* 28, *le soen penser* 52, etc. The indefinite pronoun *autrui* is found as a nominative, 1061.

Both *ke* and *de* are used to introduce the complement of a comparison, when the complement contains no verb, 684, 1084, 1411.

The plural verb always follows *gent*, 286, 625, etc.; *tute ren* 935, 'every creature, everybody', also takes a plural. Two singular subjects joined by *e* 261, etc., *u* 453, or *ne* 80, etc., have a singular verb, but after a relative referring to two singular subjects, the verb is plural, 4, 702.

Agreement of the past participle generally takes place after a direct feminine object, except *porveu* 1097 (: *fu*). Agreement with a following direct object is also found, 1057, 1080, 1182, etc., though unsupported by metre or rhyme. In four past participles conjugated with *aveir*, there is possible agreement with the subject, *passez* 698 (: *assez*), though this is perhaps an example of misdeclension, *hunie* and *ledengee* 1013 (: *changee*, fem.), *amassez* 1022 (: *assez*).[1] The apparently feminine ending *-ee* is often a graphy for *-é*, 67, 345, 697, etc.

Both the subjunctive and the indicative moods are used after *pert*, 'is manifest', subj. 102, ind. 95, and in clauses depending on a comparative, subj. 977, ind. 673, 773, 1126. In the concessive constructions *ja tant . . . ne*, *ja si . . . ne*,[2] Chardri uses the normal Old

[1] Cf. M. K. Pope and T. B. W. Reid, *The Romance of Horn* II, A.N.T.S. XII–XIII, (Oxford, 1964), 91.
[2] Cf. A. Tobler, *Vermischte Beiträge* . . . I (3rd ed., Leipzig, 1921), 136–9; O. M. Johnston, *Romanic Review* 8 (1917), 81–7.

French types with indicative, conditional or hypothetical subjunctive in the *ja*-clause, represented by *Ja tant n'averez ... Ke vers tanz maus mester n'i eit* 1591–2 (together with the anacoluthic form in which the negative subordinate clause is replaced by an affirmative principal: *ja ne fust si ben atachez Dedenz mun quor doel e tristur, Mult i avereit petit sujur* 256–8) and by *la veillesce ne passeriez mie, Ja tant ne fust duce ta vie* 597–8, as well as the juxtaposition of these two types in *ja si grant ne fust le chaut Ke nul en fust gueres grevee, Ja si chaut ne fust l'estee* 66–8 (cf. 499–502). He also uses the contaminated types with present subjunctive in the *ja*-clause, which appear to be confined to Anglo-Norman: *Ja nel pussez vus tant amer Ke vus ne truissez assez sun per* 1611–12 and *Vus serrez mort e pus porri, Ja tant suef ne seez norri* 447–8 (cf., with the clauses in the reverse order, 387–9), together with a hybrid form in which the subjunctive in the *ke*-clause is replaced by the indicative: *Ja n'eit tant oi ne tant veu Ke il ne poet estre por sot tenu* 689–90.

The indicative is also used where the subjunctive would be expected in *Veil ne jofne ne conus pas Ki n'ad mester de aucun solas* 119–20 (cf. 172, 1395; but subjunctive 165, 301, etc.); an indicative is co-ordinated with the normal subjunctive in *N'ad desuz la chape del cel Ren ke se moet u seit mortel* 1303–4; cf. also *ne sai de tuz eslire Ki meuz en vaut u seit le pire* 1603–4. An abnormal subjunctive appears in *mult ad ke li despleise* 96 and *cil ki en age gueres dure, Ke il dechece en veillesce . . .* 604–5.

A common concessive construction is that with *tut* and the subjunctive, as in *ma amie aveit . . . De tutes grace[s] a grant fuisun, Tut ne l'eust ele de aprise* 1329–31 (where Koch wrongly corrected the *eust* of *LOV* to *out*); cf. 681, 830, 1456.

In conditional sentences, the author's language includes the Anglo-Norman constructions with the verb of the *si*-clause in the future (1003), conditional (699) or present subjunctive (971, 1355, 1492, 1701). The usual form of hypothetical sentence is with the imperfect subjunctive in the protasis and the conditional in the apodosis (105–6, 142–4, 215–16, etc.), or the imperfect subjunctive in both (795–6, 797 . . . 800). The modern construction with imperfect indicative and conditional occurs only once in 231–2.

There are several anacoluthic constructions besides that in 256–8 (above); in a subordinate clause depending on a negative principal, an affirmative verb in the indicative replaces a negative verb in the subjunctive in *Un sul veillard ne vei a peine, Tant cum plus vit, plus mauz demeine* 229–30, while a negative verb in the indicative replaces an affirmative verb in the subjunctive in *tant de mei ne tendrunt cunte Ke nul ne vout sei entremettre De . . .* 654–6.

A command is in three instances expressed by the future, *prendre*[ʒ] 283, *dirreʒ* 704, 1662. The subject pronoun accompanies the imperative in *sacheʒ le vus* 240, 509, 731, 1286, etc.

A number of elliptical passages in the text suggest a certain predilection on the author's part for the infinitive, *amasser* 967, *perdre* 994 (see Notes), 1023–7 where the author changes from infinitives, *beivre, manger e vestir*, to a finite verb, *face*, then back to an infinitive *murdrir* 1027. A subject infinitive is introduced by *a* in 809 and a final infinitive by *de* in 1726, while *por* 110 is followed by a gerund where the infinitive would normally be expected (see notes on these lines).

D. *Versification*

1. *Rhyme.* The poem contains 890 couplets, 283 of which are feminine. There is one mixed rhyme, *redutee* (masc.) 755 : *espee*. There are 71 rich rhymes, 57 leonine rhymes and 31 breaks of the couplet.

2. *The Number of Syllables.* By Continental standards only 952 of the 1780 lines of the base manuscript can be considered regular octosyllabics. A comparison of all three manuscripts and the application of procedures normally used by textual editors for Anglo-Norman verse[1] show that most of the remainder were also intended to be octosyllabic, but in spite of all attempts at regularization, some of which are rather doubtful, there remain some sixty lines which are too long and about forty which are too short. At least that many again are suspect. The text has not been emended on metrical grounds.

There are 50 heptasyllabic feminine lines and a further 38 which might be made octosyllabic through the addition of a syllable from another manuscript or the assumption of hiatus between an atonic *e* and a following vowel.

The two secondary manuscripts *OV* often furnish doublets, 799, 944, etc., replacements, 314, 601, etc., or omissions, 17, 300, etc., which will permit the re-establishment of octosyllabic lines.

3. *Verse Structure.* Approximately 75 per cent of the lines have a stress accent, sometimes rather slight, on the fourth syllable, which tends to divide the line into hemistichs. In those lines where the

[1] See, for example, E. G. R. Waters, op. cit., pp. xliv–l.

accent falls on the third syllable, there are often seven, or apparently seven, syllables and in those where the fifth syllable is accented there appear to be nine. This has led me to feel that the stress rhythm of the Anglo-Norman line should not be ignored, even where one seeks a 'syllabic' solution. An approximate classification of the 1780 lines shows (i) 1330 lines with a tonic accent on the fourth syllable; this figure includes 131 lines which have a 'supernumerary' syllable after the fourth—$4 + e + 4$; (ii) 125 lines with a tonic accent on the third syllable followed by a weak e—$3 + e + 4$; (iii) 170 lines with a tonic accent on the third syllable not followed by a weak e; (iv) 160 lines with a tonic accent on the fifth syllable; (v) 95 lines where it is difficult to determine any secondary stress or hiatus.

AUTHOR

In the *Vie de seint Josaphaz* and the *Set Dormanz* the author reveals that his name is Chardri (*Jos.* 2953, *S.D.* 1892). The Abbé de la Rue attributed the *Petit Plet* also to this same Chardri in his *Archaeologia* in 1800,[1] an attribution to which no later scholars, including Koch who made a fairly thorough study of the similarities of the three poems, have seen any objections. I have re-examined the question and, although emphasizing different phonological characteristics from those Koch mentions, am also led to assume that the author of the *Petit Plet* is Chardri.

1. The three poems are all found in two manuscripts, L and O, and in each manuscript are the work of a single scribe. The order of the poems is, however, different (see Manuscripts, pp. xi–xiii), though this seems of minor importance considering the later date of O and the possibility that, as Carleton Brown suggests,[2] the scribe may have put the three French pieces together for reasons of consolidation. The study of the manuscript filiation for the *Petit Plet* has shown that O and V have a common source, Y, which is not a derivative of L. It is highly probable that this source included *Josaphaz* and the *Set Dormanz*, which would mean a fourth manuscript (besides the original and LO) where all poems were found. Yet another is possible, if we accept the existence of a faulty archetype, X, as suggested in the stemma, p. xvii.

[1] Op. cit., p. 234.　　　　[2] Op. cit., p. xxv.

2. The three works share common linguistic features. The orthography of the poems in each manuscript is the same, although Koch indicates that in *L*, the *Petit Plet* has *mult* and *avera*, etc., against *mut* and *avra* in the other two pieces. This is not quite precise because *mult* and *avereit* as well as the more frequent *mut*, *avra* may be found in *Josaphaz*. The phonology appears to be at the same point of development. Not only does one find the rhymes **ie : e** ($<$ **a**), **e** ($<$ **a**) **: ei, ai : e**, **o** checked : **o** free, **üi : ü** (see Phonology, pp. xviii–xix), but also the less usual **ai : ei**. Trethewey's study has noted[1] how these diphthongs rhyme only before final *s* and *t* in Hue de Rotelande, while in Simund de Freine the rhyme has been extended to final position and before *st, str, r, re*. In the *Petit Plet* and Chardri texts the two diphthongs rhyme in final position (*P.P.* 43, 912; *Jos.* 151, 2159, 2336; *S.D.* 1210), before *s* (*P.P.* 1120, 1629; *Jos.* 1689, 2515, 2689) and before *re, se* (*P.P.* 1216, 1295; *Jos.* 1825; *S.D.* 486). The *Set Dormanz* alone has one example before a nasal, 911. Besides being an aid to dating the text, the close similarity in the use of this rhyme can be taken as an indication of common authorship for the three works. Koch in his examination (p. xxi n.) uses the rhymes *quor : foer*, *-orie : -oire*, *-ent : -ant*, *-ur : -ür*, but these prove nothing. The *-ent : -ant* rhyme, *P.P.* 589–90, is not conclusive because *dolent* is found in rhyme with both sounds in the text (see above, p. xix), nor is the example *-ur : -ür P.P.* 1068 (see above, p. xix). *Quor : foer* is a regular rhyme at all periods, while *-orie : -oire* is orthographical.

The declension system,[2] at least among parisyllabics, is tending towards modern uniformity. In *Josaphaz* the only occurrence of *-s* in the masculine sg. nom. of parisyllabic nouns is *amis* (4 times), always in the vocative; the *Set Dormanz* has only one case of *-s*. As with the *Petit Plet*, more adjectives show *-s* in this position, 1:8 in *Josaphaz* and 1:6 in the *Set Dormanz*, as do past participles with *estre*, 1:4, 1:6. Plural nominative forms of parisyllabics have a slight predominance of *-s* in *Josaphaz*, but stand 1:2 in the *Set Dormanz* where there are only six conclusive rhymes. The choice of imparisyllabic forms would seem, as in the *Petit Plet*, to depend on rhyme or metre rather than syntactic function. The feminine *e* has not been extended to the third declension adjectives in rhyme. Analogical *e* or *s* is not present in

---

[1] Op. cit., p. xlix.
[2] For the following morphological points in the *Petit Plet*, see Morphology, pp. xx–xxii, xxiv.

first person singular present indicative forms of first or third conjugation verbs. The first person plural ending in rhyme is *-um* (: *-un*)
though the *Petit Plet*'s only rhymed example is *-uns*. Both western
and analogical imperfect endings occur in the third person singular.
The present subjunctive frequently offers *-ge*. The personal pronoun
jeo is found rhyming with *-é*. In the vocabulary Koch notes *porture*
(*Jos.* 211, 1185; *P.P.* 1441) 'bearing', *cuntrover* (*S.D.* 185; *P.P.* 662)
'invent', *bataille* (*Jos.* 1107; *P.P.* 1144) 'pain', 'fuss', *waucrant* (*Jos.*
1298; *P.P.* 1584), *murdrir* (*S.D.* 774; *P.P.* 1027) 'conceal'. The above
examples are no longer as rare as Koch believed, but from a stylistic
viewpoint they may still be regarded as valid cases of similarity.

   3. *Content and Style*. The three poems have in common a religious
and didactic tone, though the *Petit Plet* is not hagiographical material.
In each case the poet opens with a few brief remarks to the audience
on his subject and ends with an invocation of God's blessing upon
them, certainly standard procedure. In each poem the audience is
addressed as *seignurs* (*P.P.* 1; *Jos.* 2911; *S.D.* 52), which Professor Legge
suggests[1] may already have been reduced to the level of 'Ladies and
Gentlemen'. The author avoids long and tedious passages, particularly in the two shorter works (*P.P.* and *S.D.*) and makes frequent
use of proverbial and familiar phrases. Evidence of Cato's *Disticha*,
openly quoted in *P.P.* 155–6, is also found in *Jos.* 1–2 (cf. Cato,
Disticha III, 13). Perhaps more striking is the similarity in the choice
of certain phrases[2]—*E Deu nus vousist itant tenser*, *S.D.* 14, *Si Deu ne
vousist itant tenser*, *P.P.* 51; *Ki seit suz la chape deu cel*, *Jos.* 202, *N'ad
desuz la chape del cel*, *P.P.* 1303; *Ne presout mie une cenele*, *Jos.* 2081,
Ne li vaut pas une cenele, *P.P.* 970; *Austin u de seint Gregoire*, *Jos.* 7,
U seint Augustin u seint Gregoire, *P.P.* 799; *Ki le cerchast a la runde*, *Jos.*
196, *Ki les cerchast a la runde*, *P.P.* 1334 (admittedly commonplace);
En Inde n'en nule autre terre, *Jos.* 1982, *Dunc di ke Inde u la terre as Mors*,
P.P. 453. Finally compare *P.P.* 111–14 with *Jos.* 577–83:

>   Ne poet nul hoem de ceo blamer
>   Jeovene de joliveté amer:
>   Si firent tuz en lur enfance.
>   Mes suvent vent par mescheance
>   Kil le veil blasme la juvente
>   De ceo u plus mist s'entente
>   Quant esteit jovene jadis.[3]

---

[1] *Anglo-Norman Literature and its Background* (*Oxford, 1963*), p. 200.
[2] All quotations in this section and in the Notes are taken from MS. *L*.
[3] Cf. Cato, *Dist.* I, 16.

Admittedly no single item of comparison can be said to provide absolute proof of common authorship, but I feel that the marked similarity in the three areas studied suffices to allow the conclusion that Chardri is the author of the *Petit Plet*.

No precise details are known about Chardri[1] and only limited inferences can be drawn from the textual content and manuscript history. Abbé de la Rue's assignment of the poet to Gloucestershire,[2] based on the listing of a Ricardus de Chardi (not Chardri) in the *Liber Niger Scaccarii*,[3] seems, as Koch notes,[4] to be highly improbable. There would seem little doubt from his dialect and his allusions that he is English or a Norman who has chosen to live in England. He acknowledges an English proverb (ll. 1279 ff.), and states a clear preference for English women and an admiration for English knights over their French counterparts, even if he reproaches the Englishmen for their reputation as drunkards.[5] There is good reason to believe too that the Chardri poems can be situated in the west of England. Dr. Betty Hill reports that Anglicists are generally agreed that the Middle English contents of MS. *O* Part II were copied in the west.[6] The *Vie de Tobie* in *O* was written for Gwilleyme, Prior of Kenilworth in Warwickshire.[7] As for MS. *L*, it might be pointed out that the *Owl and the Nightingale*, though southern in composition, is copied in a south-western or south-west Midlands dialect,[8] while the author of the *Brut*, Layamon, was a native of Ernley near Stourport in Worcestershire.[9]

From the nature of his three works, I would agree with Miss Legge that the poet had a clerical background, though he does not use a

[1] Menger, op. cit., p. 22, n. 1, notes that A. Reimbrecht in his thesis, *Die Legende von den sieben Schläfern und der Anglo-Normannische Dichter Chardri* (Göttingen, 1880), devoted a chapter to Chardri's biography, but offered nothing new. The same can be said of the entry in J. C. Russell's *Dictionary of writers of Thirteenth Century England* (London, 1936). Professor E. G. Stanley has recently suggested to me that Chardri, a name not found elsewhere, may be an anagram of Richard.
[2] *Essais historiques sur les bardes* . . . (Caen, 1834), 3, 127.
[3] (London, 1771), p. 165.
[4] P. xx.
[5] Lines 1271–2. For a comment on this reputation, see P. Rickard, *Britain in Medieval French Literature, 1100–1500* (Cambridge, 1956), p. 167.
[6] Op. cit., p. 204; cf. Wrenn, op. cit., p. 107.
[7] Reinsch, op. cit., ll. 23 ff.; cf. Miss Hill's correction of E. W. B. Nicholson's dating quoted by Paues, op. cit., p. 222.
[8] Stanley, op. cit., pp. 17–18.
[9] N. Bøgholm, *The Layamon Texts, a Linguistical Investigation*, Travaux du cercle linguistique de Copenhague III, 5 (Copenhagen, 1944).

C

clerkly title in referring to himself,[1] while his cheerful and often lyrical style suggests the skills of a *jongleur* or a travelling preacher.[2]

DATE

The content of the *Petit Plet* gives no hint of the date of the poem's composition. The linguistic evidence, however, will allow a closer estimate than is possible from dating the oldest manuscript L. Various editors of the *Owl and the Nightingale* and palaeographers place L in the first half of the thirteenth century, possibly near 1250 according to Mr. N. R. Ker,[3] but the consensus from internal evidence in other items in the manuscript is that the poem itself must have been composed between 1189 (the death of Henry II) and 1216 (the beginning of the reign of Henry III).[4] Layamon's *Brut* was probably written before 1189.[5] The *terminus ad quem* of 1216 suggested for the manuscript derives from the abrupt termination of the Anglo-Norman chronicle on the English kings at folio 232v with the words:

Aprés Richard si regna Johan sun frere ki dunat a tuz iurs mes de Engletere cruel triu a Rume. En sun tens fu perdue Normandie. Aprés la mort cestu rei Johan si regna sun fiz Henri.

The rest of the page is already ruled and remains blank, as though the author or scribe intended to continue. No mention is made of the regents William Marshall (d. 1219) or Hubert de Burgh, who governed England until the beginning of Henry's personal reign in 1227, nor is there any further record of Henry himself. This could indicate that the manuscript was copied near this time (1216), but it is equally possible that the scribe was copying from an incomplete work, or interrupted his task for some reason.

The linguistic characteristics of the *Petit Plet* allow a tentative dating near the turn of the twelfth century. Following Prof. Trethewey's study of the *ai* : *ei* rhymes,[6] we can place the *Petit Plet* very near or even before the works of Simund de Freine which Matzke judges to be near 1200. Part of Matzke's own proof, however, is this

---

[1] *Op. cit.*, p. 193; cf. *Anglo-Norman in the Cloisters* (Edinburgh, 1950), p. 201.

[2] Koch, p. xxiv, mentions the possibility that Chardri was a Goliard and points out too his use of chivalric allusions.

[3] Op. cit., p. ix.   [4] Stanley, op. cit., p. 19.

[5] Bøgholm, op. cit., p. 9.   [6] Op. cit., pp. xlviii–l; cf. above, p. xviii.

very similarity of the two authors. The *ai* : *ei* rhymes are not as restricted in Chardri as in Hue de Rotelande's *Protheselaus* (1174–90),[1] nor are they extended to as many positions as in Frère Angier (1212)[2] or the *Petite Philosophie*.[3] They are if anything slightly more conservative than in Simund de Freine where the rhyme is found before *st*, *stre*, *r*, as well as in the positions noted for the *Petit Plet* (see Phonology, p. xviii). The rhyming of infinitives in *-eir* with *-er* makes the *Petit Plet* later than the *St. Catherine* (one doubtful example),[4] while the absence of analogical feminine *e* and of *e* in the first person sg. pres. ind. of the first conjugation (both, incidentally, lacking in de Freine) make our text more conservative than Angier, though no conclusive evidence of these two traits is found in the *Petite Philosophie*. The general similarity with the de Freine texts, despite the uncertainty of linguistic dating in Anglo-Norman and despite Matzke's general estimate of the date of de Freine's works, leads me to conclude that the *Petit Plet* was written in the later years of the twelfth century or the early years of the thirteenth.

SOURCES

It is perhaps imprecise to speak of sources for the *Petit Plet*. Chardri owes his inspiration to more than one author, while his method of presentation, particularly in reversing the usual debating rôles of the old man and the youth, the lyrical or humorous development of certain passages, and his extensive use of proverbial material, make the work a very original and personal one. The poem contains only one explicit reference to a source, Cato, author of the *Disticha*, who is mentioned in l. 154 with a quotation following which recalls Distich III, 6.[5] Further possible influences of Cato may be noted in reference to youth and old age (I, 16), death (I, 22; II, 3; IV, 22), ill words of others (III, 2), poverty (I, 21; IV, 1; IV, 16; IV, 35), generosity (III, 9), caution (I, 2; IV, 28), women (III, 12), friendship (I, 23). But if there are many details which recall Cato, it is evident that in structure the debate is more indebted to *De remediis fortuitorum*,

---

[1] Ed. Franz Kluckow (Göttingen, 1924), pp. 2, 54 ff.
[2] M. K. Pope, *Etude sur la langue de frère Angier* (Paris, 1903), p. 10.
[3] Pp. xxix–xxxi.
[4] Ed. W. MacBain, A.N.T.S. XVIII (Oxford, 1964), p. xxi.
[5] J. W. Duff and A. M. Duff, *Minor Latin Poets* (Loeb Classical Library) (London and Cambridge, Mass., 1934).

sometimes attributed to Seneca,[1] which is a dialogue between Sensus and Ratio on the vicissitudes of life. The debt is especially clear from l. 289 on where the older man begins his series of plaints. The *De remediis* dialogue deals, as does the *Petit Plet*, with death, death by violence, death in a foreign country, death before one's time or without burial; with sickness; with other men's ill opinions of oneself; with poverty, grief, loss of fortune and lack of power, and finally with the loss of children, friend and wife. In this last of the ascending order of griefs, the *Petit Plet* lists the loss of wife as less dolorous than the loss of a true friend, and the poet has harmed the balance of his work with his long diatribe against women. The replies, too, reflect the influence of the Latin work. Death, says Ratio, is the natural course of man; life is but a pilgrimage; it is best to die while enjoying life; after death there is no feeling; sickness is a test of strength, a battle; speakers of evil are themselves evil; any country can be one's home; men were born poor; money loses its owner as its owner does it; children are not one's own but gifts of fortune; another friend can be found; one should be ashamed of having but one; a good wife would have changed; another as good can be found. In addition to the *De remediis* and the *Disticha*, Chardri is drawing from that wider source Mrs. Crosland calls 'The Wisdom Literature of the Middle Ages'[2] of which Seneca and Cato are part. There is a whole current of didactic and semi-religious material, as well as the usual hagiographical and biblical texts, where the subjects debated in the *Petit Plet* are encountered. Boethius and Job are two examples, and these may well have provided Chardri with inspiration. One can hardly say that the satirical attack against women can be attributed to a single author, though it is certain that the attitudes of Theophrastus and St. Jerome were not unfamiliar to Chardri. Koch notes (p. xix) the similarity with Theophrastus' *Liber aureolus de nuptiis* cited by Jean de Meung in the *Roman de la Rose*.[3] All that remains of this work is an extract inserted by St. Jerome in his treatise *Adversus Jovinianum*[4] and reproduced by John of Salisbury

---

[1] Abel Bourgéry discusses the question of attribution in *Sénèque Prosateur* (Paris, 1922), pp. 69–70. The Latin text is reproduced by F. Haase, *Senecae Opera* (Leipzig, 1852–3), III, 446–57, and R. G. Palmer, *Seneca's 'De remediis fortuitorum' and the Elizabethans* (Chicago, 1953).

[2] J. Crosland, *Medieval French Literature* (Oxford, 1956), p. 33.

[3] Ed. E. Langlois, S.A.T.F. (1914–24), III, ll. 8561 ff; ed. F. Lecoy, C.F.M.A. 95, II, ll. 8531 ff.

[4] *Sancti Eusebii Hieronymi Stridonensis Presbyteri Operum* (Paris, 1706), IV, 144–228.

in his *Polycraticus*.[1] Here it is recommended that a man should only take a wife if she is beautiful, of good conduct, born of upright parents, and if the man himself is both rich and healthy. A woman will demand fine clothes, gold, jewels, servants and will protest if she finds the neighbour's wife better dressed than she. Koch also notes a resemblance with Goliard poetry.[2] Furthermore Chardri liberally inserts proverbs and aphorisms, which substantiate my impression that the *Petit Plet* is much more than an academic re-working of other writers' ideas.

ESTABLISHMENT OF THE TEXT

As noted above (p. xv), the choice of *L* as base manuscript presents no problems. The text presented is as it appears in *L*, except for rare emendations demanded by the context. All departures from the base manuscript are given separately and without siglum at the foot of the text, while the variants of MSS. *O* and *V* are listed together below these rejected readings. All variants affecting sense and metre have been recorded in this list and I have also considered it useful to include rare spellings and forms, especially those reflect-ing insular characteristics. Where both *O* and *V* have the same variant, the spelling follows the one whose siglum is given first. I have indicated in the variant readings where the scribe clearly distinguishes *v* and *u*. The square brackets between ll. 1710–61 indicate lacunae caused by wear to the last folio. Elsewhere square brackets denote additions or completions to the text based on *O* and *V*. Occasionally these are orthographical emendations made to facilitate comprehen-sion, e.g. *must[r]er* 294, *girra[i]* 623. In cases where the meaning is clear, I have preferred to leave the original spellings, e.g. *serrer* 1457. In general, the word division of the scribe has been followed, but before vowels *al*, etc., have been written *a l'*, etc., while words such as *desoremés, nunchaleir, tresduz, demaleire* (cf. *demaleires* 1243) have been written as single items as there seems to be no fixed scribal pattern. Because of their infrequency, *fous large* 962, *foularge* 979 and *fors parti* 1140 have been left as they stand. Confusion between *t* and *c* is frequent, but I have attempted in each instance to distinguish the

[1] C. C. J. Webb, *Joannis Saresberiensis Episcopi Carnotensis Polycraticus* (Oxford, 1909), VIII, xi, 294 ff.

[2] P. xix; in this respect note 'Golias de conjuge non ducenda' among the *Latin poems commonly attributed to Walter Mapes*, ed. Thomas Wright (London, 1841), p. 77.

letter intended by the scribe. In the transcription, distinction is made
between *i* and *j*, *c* and *ſ* and the acute accent employed to differentiate
é from atonic *e* in final syllables. The divisions of the poem are made
where there is a change in speaker. Where the marginal indications
of such changes, *L'enfant* or *Le veillard* (usually *veill;* in the MS.) are
lacking, I have inserted the appropriate heading in square brackets.
All headings have been centred. Modern capitalization and punctua-
tion are introduced according to standard editorial practice. The
double letter *ff*, *ffors* 1271, *ffēme* 1299, etc., which is used at the
beginning of the line, is transcribed as *F*.

ICI COMENCE LE PETIT PLET

Beau duz seignurs, por vus dedure
Vus cunterai un esveisure
De un veillard e de un enfant
4 Ki se entredalierent tant
De juvente e de veillesce,
De jolifté e de peresce.
Chescun mustra sa grevance,
8 Sa eise u sa mesestance:
Si fu le estrif mult delitius
Del veillart e del jofne tus.
Si est appelé le PETIT PLET
12 Icest tretiz ke ci est fet.
Grant solaz est a feble curage
Ki s'esmaie de un ventage,
Car mult i ad verraiz respiz
16 De ben assis e de bonz diz.
Ore entendez, si les orrez ben,
Ke jeo ne ment de nule ren,
Car en jovene poet l'em veer
20 Suventefeiz mult grant saver.

Un vaslet, ki mult esteit pensif
E de divers pensers sutif,
S'esbaneout par aventure
24 Por joie aver e enveisure
E por eschivre la ren del mund
Ke plus le cors de home cunfund:
Ceo est tristur ke Deu maudie,
28 Ki tut hunist la nostre vie.
Mes trestuz ceus met jeo defors
Ki le quor unt trublé od le cors

Incipit Ici cumence le petyt ple entre le juvencel e le veylard *O*; Ci commence le peti
plee *V*   1 vus de d. *V*   2 cutrey *O*; enueysure *OV*   10 De v., iuuentus *V*
14 senmaye *O*, se maye *V*   17 si oiez ben *O*; les *not in V*   18 *a second* rien *in
right margin V*   20 suventfoyz *V*; mult *not in OV*   21 Un iuuencel *O*   22 E de
uers p. *O*

Par malvesté de male gent,
32 U ceus ki amur certein esprent;
Ceus ne blam pas, car de l'autrui
Apernent quanke il unt de ennui,   249c
Mes papelarz e les coveitus,
36 Les surquidez, les envius,
Li faus sutif e li leres,
Li faus pleidur e li tricheres,
E tuz iceus ki unt penser
40 Par mal de lur proeme enginner.
Si il ne pensent si de ceo nun,
Deu lur doint sa maleisun.
Li vaslet dunt si tuché vus ai
44 Mult fu pensif, ne sai de quai;
Mes por tolir mauveis penser
Se mist tut sul en un verger,
E diseit ben ke ja dolur
48 N'avereit en sun quor sujur
De cest mund ki vent e vet,
E ke ja ne rendreit plet
Si Deu ne[l] vousist itant tenser
52 Ke amendast le soen penser,
Penser ne vout si de lui nun:
Ore li doint Deu sa beneisun.
Par le verger e sa e la
56 Icest vaslet itant ala
Ke il choisi une funtaine
Dunt l'ewe esteit e clere e seine.
La surse esteit e nette e bele
60 Ke rouleout cele gravele,
Si fu la noise duce e sutive,
Si resemblout ben chose vive.
Trestut entur fu l'erbe drue
64 Estencelee de flur menue,
E si esteint li arbre haut,

---

32 c. en prent *V*   33 b. io pas ke de a. *V*   35 le c. *V*   36 e les e. *V*
39 unt] un *V*   41 si ke de ceo *O*   43 Le iuuencel *O*   44 fu *not in V*
50 tendreyt *V*   51 ne *OV*   55 le verge ca e la *V*   56 iuuencel *O*   58 esteyt
c. e s. *O*   59 esteyt n. e b. *OV*   64 des flurs menue *V*

Ke ja si grant ne fust le chaut
Ke nul en fust gueres grevee,
68 Ja si chaut ne fust l'estee.
Les oiseals de meinte manere
Se acosteient a la rivere;
Por le verdur e por la flur
72 Mult chantoient a grant duçur.
Le vaslet de ceo mult s'esjoi
E del duz chant ke il oi,
E mut li heita plus le liu
76 Ke meint riche hume sun riche fiu.

L'ENFANT

Li vaslet sist desus la rive
Por aviser la surse naive,
Si en out al quor joie si grant
80 Ke unkes reis ne quens n'out tant.
Atant survint un veil veillard
Ki li veneit de l'autre part,
De pensers murnes e tant dolent
84 Ke al vis li pareit sun mautalent.
Avant passa, si vit l'enfant
Icele grant joie demenant,
E cil se estut, si se apua
88 Sur sun bastun, si li salua.
Le vaslet li respundi en haut:
'Sire pruedom, ke Deu vus saut.
Ore ven seer ci pres de mei,
92 Si me cuntez de cel effrei
Por quei demenez itel dolur.
Mult pert ben en ta colur
Ke tun quor n'est pas a eise
96 E ke mult ad ke li despleise.'

L'enfant *is beside l.* 77   87 si] sil   93 icel

67 nul i fust *OV*   69 oisil *V*   73 ieouencel *O*, mult *not in O*; senioie *V*   74 oye *V*
75 plus liu *OV*   76 Ke meint h. *O*; si r. f. *V*   77 iuuencel *O*   78 la s. vyue *OV*
79 en le q. *O*, el q. *V*   83 tant *not in O*   84 Kel v. *OV*   87 Icil si tust si se pua
O; Icil se tuit si sa pua *V*   88 li] la *O*, le *V*   89 iuuencel *O*; Li v.r. *V*

LE VEILLARD

'Certes ceo est veir,' fet li veillart,
'Mult sui pensif, si Deu me gart,
E mei merveil estrangement
100   Ke point n'avez de mun marrement,   250a
Einz si grant joie si demenez.
Ben pert ke poi seez senez,
Ke vus vus bainet en cest delit
104   Ki mult vus endurra petit.
Si vus seussez ceo ke jeo pens,
Aillur turneriez le vostre sens.'

L'ENFANT

'Sire prudom,' fet li vaslet,
108   'Mult me acupez de estrange ret,
Ke jeo m'en vois si desportant
Por mun quor recunfortant.
Si jofne aime l'enveisure,
112   Fors ke trop n'i eit desmesure,
Ne devez trop blamer sa entente:
Si feistes vus en ta juvente.
Custume est de veille gent,
116   Quant lur bel age les susprent,
Ke il trestut turnent a rage
Quanke il amerent en lur jofne age.
Veil ne jofne ne conus pas
120   Ki n'ad mester de aucun solas.'

LE VEILLARD

'Vaslet,' fet cil, 'par un bon mestre
Uncore porriez saives estre.
Car ben est veirs ke tu me dis
124   Ke jeo esteie jolif jadis,

97 est *not in* V   100 martyrement O   101 g. ioie d. O   104 Ke vus mut e. V
105 s. ore ceo ke O   106 le *not in* OV   107 iuuencel O   108 mencupez OV;
de e. apel O   111 l' *not in* V   117 en r. O   118 lur *not in* OV   119 cunust O
121 Iouencel fet il O   122 sauuez e. O, sages e. V   123 Ke bien V

Mes cum plus entrai en age,
Tant tornai plus a grant folage
Mes enfances e mun enveisure,
128 Car illurs avei turné ma cure.
De ben vivere e de ma fin
Tant en pensai seir e matin
Ke tut me turna a grant ennui
132 La grant joie u jo tant fu.'

L'ENFANT

'Sire,' fet dunc li juvencel,
'Icest penser fu bon e bel,
De ben vivere fet bon penser,
136 De ben morir e a Deu aler.   250b
De trop duleir n'i vei resun
Fors as veus ki sunt de sesun
De tost morir, si il unt esté
140 Tute lur vie en mauvesté:
Cil deivent dolur aver adés.
Si jeo preisse le secle trop a fes,
Ke tant sui jofnes e leger,
144 Jo me porreie tant charger
De tant penser e tant duleir
Ke jo cherreie en nunpoier.
Mult tost chanu en devendreie,
148 E pus aprés mult tost porreie
Par teu dolur haster ma fin.
E ceo serreit un faus latin,
Si averei perdu par grant musage
152 Tute la meité de mun age.
Ben savez cum il est escrit,
Si cum Catun enseinne e dit:
"Entremedlez vostre cure
156 De joie u de aukun enveisure."
Por ceo ne vus esmerveillez

126 grant *not in* O   127 men enueysure O, menveisure V   131 tut *not in* O
137 veie O, ne vei V   138 a v. OV   142 Si joe i p. V   144 purray O
146 en un poeir O   153 s. kil est e. OV   154 e *not in* V   157 enmerveyllez OV

Si jeo sui joius e lez,
Assez porra venir li tens
160 Ke penser puis de autre sens.'

LE VEILLARD

'Par Deu,' fet li prudom, 'beau fiz,
Ben savez afficher vos diz,
A dire quanke al quor vus gist.
164 N'ad suz cel ren ke Deu fist
Ke seur vus en peust fere
De ta vie u de autre affere,
Tant sumes fresles e cheitifs:
168 Mar vint l'ure ke fumes vifs.
Por ceo teng jo a grant folie
De promettre mult lunge vie.
Car n'ad suz cel veillard ne enfant
172 Ke set l'ure del moriant,   250c
Car ausi tost moert li letanz
Cum celui ki ad cent anz.
Por ceo sui mult pensif e murne
176 Del mund ki vet e pus returne
E sa e la e munt [e] jus:
Mult en poet hoem estre cunfus.
Pensez en, si fras ke sage,
180 Lessez folie e tun musage.'

L'ENFANT

'Sire,' fet l'enfant adunkes,
'Ki sarmoner ne seust unkes,
Vus le porriez a ceo mettre
184 Sanz abecé e tut sanz lettre,
Tant avez la lange pleine
Des diz le prestre al dimeine.
Ben dites veir ke jo pleggage

158 Si ore su *OV*; ieofnes e l. *O*   159 A ces p. *OV*; avenir *V*   163 a q. *V*
165 pot *V*   170 pᵉmettre *O*; mult *not in* *V*   173 autre si t. meorent *O*; morent *V*
179 P. einz *V*; frez *O*, fres *V*   181 a idunkes *O*   182 sustes *V*   183 purrez *OV*
184 abett *V*   186 De d. au p. de d. *O*; De d. au p. *V*   187 ieo de pl. *O*

188 Nen ai pas de mun jofne age,
     Mes cil haut rei ke nus tuz fist
     Ja por duleir un jur de respit
     Ne vus dorra, sachez de fi,
192 Si tu ne l'as de plus servi.
     E si jo moer jofnes enfant,
     Meuz voil aler a Deu riant
     Ke veuz chanu a chef de tur
196 Finir ma vie a grant dolur.
     Car jo vus di, cum home plus vit,
     Plus maus atent e meins delit,
     Car veillesce ad iteu manere
200 Ki plus avance, plus met arere;
     Cum plus les ad mis en age,
     Tant lur ad fet greinnur damage,
     Car anguisses i troverunt
204 E gueres pru ne i s'eiderunt.
     Por maladies e por ennui
     Servi cuvent k'il seient de autrui,
     Cum norice fet sun enfant,
208 E sa e la vet danzelant
     Por le cucher e le lever   250d
     E le manger e le plurer.
     Tut issi cuvent aprés
212 Servir les veuz desoremés.
     Tant redotent en nunsaveir
     K'il ne poent lur sen aveir;
     Dunt,' fet il, 'freie musardie
216 Si m'estuasse a tele vie.
     Meus me vaut mort ke vif
     Ke jo fusse un tel cheitif,
     Ke ore apreisse la dolur
220 Ke dunc me serreit a gref sojur;
     E jo mettreie en nunchaler

196 Finit   200 Kil   206 servir

189 haut *not in* V; nus] vus O 190 dolur O 193 morre V 196 Finer V
200 Kil O; Ke plus a. V 202 grant d. V 204 p. ni prendrunt OV 206 ke
vent, seit O 212 veuz *not in* V 214 pussent V 216 cele v. O
217 uaudreit OV 221 m. a n. OV

La joie ke Deu me fet ore aver
Por lui servir, si cum li plest,
224 E jo le freie od grant deshet,
Par orgoil u par melancolie;
Dunc me doint Deu mult curte vie.
Meus vaut jofne morir a joie
228 Ke veuz veillard a male voie.
Un sul veillard ne vei a peine,
Tant cum plus vit, plus mauz demeine,
E cum serreit en joie dunkes,
232 Si en avant ne l'aveit unkes?
Mes trestut ad despendu sun age
En dolur e en mal usage.
Ben sachez ke l'en troeve escrit,
236 Dunt meint en poet aver respit:
Ki a Deu dune ceo ke li plest,
Si a bon quor e a joie nel fet,
Ja n'en avera merci ne gré,
240 Sachez le vus por verité.
Ore poez avant passer
E un autre jofne entasser
De vos paroles, si beau vus est—
244 De l'encuper estes tut prest;
Si mei lessez des ore ester,
Sanz nul ennui ici juer.'   251a

LE VEILLARD

Li veus hoem dunc li respund:
248 'Si Deu me saut, ki fist le mund,
Mult quidez estre sutil e beaut
De un sen ke mult poi vus vaut.
Porreit l'en en nule guyse
252 Tun quor changer de cest emprise

251 porriet

224 fray *V*   226 doyne d. *V*; mult *not in O*   228–9 *telescoped* Ke veu veillard ne
veye a poine *O*   232 en nauant *V*   235 en escrit *O*   236 en *not in O*; prendre
r. *OV*   237 ke il pl. *V*   238 Si ad b. q. *V*   239 en *not in V*   244 est uus p. *V*
246 e. e si j. *V*   247 dunc *not in OV*   248 Si d. me gart *OV*; tut le m. *O*
249 baud *OV*   250 mult *not in OV*   251 Purreyt *OV*   252 Tun q. charger *O*

Ke ussez occupé ta cure
En tristur plus ke en enveisure?'

L'ENFANT

'Nenal,' fet cil, 'ben le sachez
256 Ke ja ne fust si ben atachez
Dedenz mun quor doel e tristur,
Mult i avereit petit sujur,
Tant me sai jo ben cunforter,
260 Si sai a mun quor ben porter
Ke ja ne i vendra fors joie e ben,
Ja ne i demorra mauveise ren.'

LE VEILLARD

Li prudum dist: 'Vaslet, a certes
264 Mult vus en porreient venir granz pertes
Ke teu chose alissez vantant,
Dunt ne fussez espruvee avant.
Mes si il vus fust ore a pleisir,
268 U vus eussez nul bon leisir,
Jo me serreie ci pres de vus.
Sanz ceo k'il n'i eust curuz
Ne mauvesté ne vilanie,
272 Vus demandereie de vostre vie
Aventures ke suvent venent,
Ki quor de home trublent e tenent,
Saver mun, si solacer
276 Nus en pussez de aukun penser.'

L'ENFANT

'Jeo le grant,' fet li vaslet, 'beau sire,

L'enfant *is beside l. 255*   260 sui, bon   277 Ieo li g.

254 en *not in* V   255 fet il V   256 ne *not in* O   258 p. sauur O   260 sui O,
sai V   261 v. si ioie OV   262 maveisie V   264 porreit V; granz *not in* O
267 il *not in* V   268 nul *not in* OV; leiser V   269 serrey si pris de O; serrai V
270 il *not in* OV   274 Li q. V   277 Oy grant, iuuencel O

Ke vus pussez tun vuleir dire.
Ja curucee ne mei verrez,
280 Ne, si Deu plest, vus ne serrez.
E vus freez une curteisie:
Si jo vus di sen u folie,   *251b*
Tut le prendre[z] uelement,
284 Car ceo affert a sage gent;
Si jofne enfant de ren mesdit,
Ne deivent plet tenir, ceo quit.
Comencez dunc,' fet li vaslet,
288 'Sen u folie, quel ke vus plet.'

LE VEILLARD

'Certes,' fet cil, 'mult bonement;
Mes jeo vei ci tut erraument
Venir tantes aventures
292 Ki felunesses sunt e dures,
Ke jo ne sai u comencer,
E tutes ne puis jo pas must[r]er.
Une a primes vus nomerai,
296 Ceo est le tut: ke jo morrai.
Sachez, par el passer ne puis,
De ceo al quor sui trop cunfus.'

L'ENFANT

Fet li vaslet: 'Par seint Richer,
300 Unc n'oi mes hoem si comencer
Ki de la cue feist le chef.
Ore vus dirrai cuntre cest gref:
La mort ke tant est redutee
304 Ne deit pas peine estre nomee,
Ne survenue de malaventure,
Einz est tut dreit curs de Nature.

298 fui

281 frez *O*   283 Tut] Tant *OV*; prendez *O*   286 Nen *O*   289 fet il *OV*
294 En tutes, muser *V*   295 Unes *V*   299 iuuencel *O*   300 mes *not in OV*
301 feyt *O*, fest *V*   302 co gr. *V*

Si Nature vus est encuntre quor,
308 Dunt sai jo ben, en memes le foer
Tei deit ennuer ta bele vie,
Ben le sachez, mes nel fet mie;
Car si grant dreit avez en mort
312 Cum de vivre en grant desport.'

[LE VEILLARD]

'Ben est veir, mes mult me meot,
Fet li veillart, morir m'estoet.'

[L'ENFANT]

'Prudum, fet cil, por ceo nasquistes,
316 Nul ne serra de ceo quites.
Quanke s'e[n] vent, pus s'en revet;
A quei dunkes fetes teu plet?'   251c

[LE VEILLARD]

'Beau fiz,' fet il, 'jo dut la mort,
320 Si ne pus aver cunfort.'

[L'ENFANT]

L'enfant respund: 'Ceo n'est pas sens
De trop duleir e perdre tens.'
E pus ad dit: 'Ceo est grant folie
324 De duter tant en ceste vie
La ren ke ja ne poet faillir,
Ceo est de tost u tart morir.
Ki dute ceo ke failler ne poet,
328 De mult petite chose se moet.

314 mort

309 dei OV   312 g. cunfort O   315 P. pur ceo fet cil n. OV; fest V   320 nen
p. O   321 co ne pas V   322 dolier O   325 put V   327 faillir OV

D

Cil ki nasqui, aprés morra,
Passer par el pas ne porra.'

LE VEILLARD

  Li veus prudum adunc li dist:
332 'Assis avez ben cest respit,
  E ceo me fet grant joie aver
  Ke si jofne estes de grant saver.
  Solaz en ai, mes nekedent
336 Plus vus dirrai de mun talent
  Por plus oir de vos bons diz;
  De grant solaz estes, beau fiz.
  Morir m'estoet certes, beau frere.'

L'ENFANT

340 'Est ceo dunc sen,' fet il, 'beau pere,
  Ke vus dutez itant la mort,
  Si ne vuler aver cunfort,
  Mes tuz jurs dites ke vus morrez?
344 Cument dunc passer porrez
  Le gué ke tant ad esté usee?
  Ben ne serra ja encusé,
  Mes tuz jurs mal, quanke l'en poet:
348 A mauveis hoem dire l'estoet.
  Ore moergez vus u u demain,
  Ne estes pas le premerein
  Ne le drein ne serrez pas.
352 A quei estes dolent e las?
  Tuz sunt partiz quanke furent,
  Reis, emperus, trestuz morirent,   251d
  E tuz iceus ki vendrunt aprés
356 De la mort en porterunt le fes.
  Dame Nature, quant vus nasquistes,

---

334 Ki *L'enfant is in left-hand margin, beside l. 340*

329 Cil ki vendra *V* 331 veus *not in V* 333 E *not in O* 334 Ki *O* 340 Est
ceo dute *V*; sen *not in V*; sent, fet a *O* 342 uolez *OV* 345 Le ieu *OV* 350
Nen *O* 351 le *not in V* 354 mururent *O*, murent *V*

Tes jurneies ad tutes escrites
E meintenant mist a ta vie
360 Un terme ke vus ne passerez mie.
Tant cum estes en cest estage,
Ta vie n'est fors un pelrimage,
E au derein repeirerez
364 A ta nature, kar vus morrer.'

[LE VEILLARD]

'Ceo est ceo ke jeo vus di,'
Fet li prudum, 'dunt sui marri.'

[L'ENFANT]

'N'ad suz cel hoem,' fet il, 'beau sire,
368 Ke en repruver vus peust dire
Ke vus morrez u tost u tart,
K'il n'en eust aukes sa part;
Quant le fiz Deu suffri la mort,
372 Si vus la dutez, ceo est a tort.'

LE VEILLARD

'Ben est veirs,' fet il, 'beau fiz,
Grant folie est sulum vos diz
De trop duter u loinz u pres,
376 Quant tuz portent mesmes le fes.
Mes jeo pens mult de quele mort
L'em peust aver greinnur cunfort.
Si jo receuse mutes colees
380 De hache u de cops de espees,
U fusse detrenché menuement,
Ceo mei serreit un gref turment.'

360 ni p. *V*   362 for cum un p. *O*; ne fors *V*   364 *not in V*; murrez *O*; a terre; par aillours ne chaperetz *in the right-hand margin V*   366 dune su mar cy *O* 367 fet il *not in OV*   368 poet *O*   369 murriez *V*   372 a *not in O*   375 De trop aler *OV*   377 mut deske la mort *O*   378 put *V*   378–9 *Between these lines* Murir mestet certes beu frere *O* (cf. l. 339); Morir mestut certes bieau frere/Mes io ne say en quele manere *V*

L'ENFANT

Le vaslet adunc li respund:
384 'Si Deu mei gard, ki fist le mund,
Jo vus en dirrai mun avis
De ceo ke ci me avez requis:
Ja tant ne seez en pes u en guerre
388 Plaé par arme ke seit en terre,
Ne perdrez fors par une la vie.
Dunt di jo ben ke ceo est folie,   252a
Si Jesu set ke il morra par plaie,
392 Si il de plusurs plaies s'esmaie.
Car une mortele autant li frat
Cum cinc cenz autres, si il les ad.
Por ceo, sire, ja ne pensez,
396 Quant vus savez ke morir devez.
Lessez celui a cunvenir
Ki cel e terre poet tut tenir
E fere de tut sa volunté,
400 Ke il vus guie par sa pieté.
E si facez vus un saveir:
Lessez ester icest duleir,
Kar ja por itel affere
404 Ne cunquerrez plein pé de terre.'

LE VEILLARD

'Ben est veirs,' fet il, 'beau frere;
Beneite seit icele mere
Ki fist itele porteure,
408 Ki dire set iteu mesure.
Mes une ren,' fet il, 'desplet,
Ke mult mun quor met en dehet.
Ore vus dirrai le men corage:

411 d. ke mun c.

383 iuuencel *O*   384 tut le m. *O*   385 en *not in OV*; men *O*   386 requis] apris *V*
390 est *not in V*   391 Si home set *OV*   392 il *not in V*; sen maie *V*   393 atant *V*
395 nen p. *OV*   396 vus *not in OV*   398 put *V*   400 Kuil (?) *V*; pité *OV*
403 Que, pur nul a. *V*   408 sust *O*, sout *V*   409 fe il *O*   410 mult *not in O*
411 d. men c. *O*

412 Ke si jo vois en pelrimage,
    Si me vendra une maladie,
    Poet cel estre, ki me tout la vie,
    Si serrai en estrange pais
416 Mult esgaré, ceo me est avis,
    E sanz amis e sanz aie
    M'en partirai de ceste vie;
    Si en serra ma dolur grant
420 En vie e al muriant.
    U si jeo moerc u si jeo vif,
    Si serra[i] un dolerus cheitif,
    Kar loinz serrai de mun pais,
424 Trop esgaré sanz mes amis,
    E de mei nul plet ne frunt
    Les estranges ki mei verrunt.'   252b

L'ENFANT

    'Beaus sire,' fet dunc l'enfant,
428 'De ceo ke vus alez dementant
    Por aventures ke trop avenent,
    Ki en amertume tun quor tenent,
    De ceo ne mei merveil pas.
432 Mes si tant estes dolent e las
    Ke de cunfort n'avez cure,
    Ceo est la greinnure mesaventure;
    Kar si vus alez en estrange terre,
436 En pelrimage u en autre affere,
    Ben deit ta discretiun
    Tun jofne quor mettre a reisun.
    Jofne quor vus apeau jeo,
440 Ki creit itute volunté.
    Un sages hoem e de bel age
    Suzdure poet un fou curage.
    Ore moergez u ke ceo seit,
444 Tun pais ert e a bon dreit;

421 moert

414 Put *V*   420 el m. *O*, en le m. *V*   421 meor *O*, mor *V*; vifs *V*   422 serra *V*
431 mei *not in O*; merveylle *O*   440–567 *a folio is missing in O*

Tun cors est terre e a terre irras;
Dunc di jo ben, sachez sanz gas,
Vus serrez mort e pus porri,
448   Ja tant suef ne seez norri.
A mei serreit dunc fort affere
Ta char sevrer hors de la terre,
Kar ne saverei le quel est tel,
452   Ne ne savereit nul hoem mortel.
Dunc di ke Inde u la terre as Mors
Est si naturele a tun cors
Cum la terre u vus nasquites;
456   Ja ne serrez de ceo quites.
Sachez ke dunc est musardie
De trop penser en ceste vie
U vus voillez de ci partir
460   E u te faces ensevelir.
L'em dort si suef en autre pais
Cum en sun propre, ceo m'est avis.'   252c

LE VEILLARD

'Ben est veir,' fet li veillart,
464   'Mes dites mei, si Deu vus gart,
Ore seit ke ne moere mie,
Coment demenerai jo ma vie
Sanz dolur e sanz tristesce?
468   Si jo sent mal u nule destresce
Par aventure en estrange terre,
Si jo i vois por mun meuz fere,
A ki pleindre ne saverei pas;
472   De ceo serrei dolent e las,
Kar mes amis ne verrei mie
Ki me soleient fere cumpainie.
Cument ke seit, de mun dehet
476   Les estranges ne tendrunt plet.
Ceo me serreit un gref penser

460 esisevelir

451 Ki ne s. *V*   453 a M. *V*   459 U *not in V*   466 demerrai *V*   471 neuerrai
pas *V*   472 serrai *V*   473 a. ni v. *V*

Dunt jo porreie mult doluser.'
Li veil se tint e ne dist mes,
480 Por escuter se tint en pes.
Ben aparceit e set l'enfant
Ke cil l'i vet mult agueitant,
U par fet u par aukun dit
484 Ke il l'i trublast un petit,
Ke sa joie peust desdire
E sa emprise descunfire.

L'ENFANT

'Sire,' fet l'enfant, 'a certes,
488 Ore vei ben ke mutes pertes
Vus poent avenir tute jur
Ke vus meissent en grant dolur.
Si femme fussez u enfant,
492 Meins vus porreie blamer de tant
Ke tun quor fust si volage
Ke doleir vousist por teu damage.
Ore vus dirrai le men avis:
496 Ja ne serrez en teu pais
Ke le vostre ne seit sanz faille,
Si vus ne valez une maille;   252*d*
Ja tant ne saverez par terre errer
500 Ke cil ki fist e cel e mer
Ne vus veie e tost e tart,
Ja nen irrez icele part.
Ceo est cil ki fist communement
504 E terre e mer e cel e vent,
E tut le fist por vus servir,
Si vus le sussez recuillir.
U ke vus seez tresturné,
508 Trestut vus serrat besturné,
Sachez le vus ben por veir,

498 ne] en

478 purrai *V* 482 cil le v. *V* 484 Ke le t. *V* 490 meitent a g. d. *V*
492 purrei b. di tant *V* 497 le *not in V* 498 ne] en *V* 499 tant *not in V*
502 Ia ni i. *V* 507 E ke *V*

Si vus ne fetes sun vuleir.
Neis en la mesun vostre pere
512   De parent n'averez ne de mere
Joie parfite ne nul aie,
Si vus ne servez le fiz Marie.
Kar dunc vus cuntralierunt
516   Tuz iceus ki sunt al mund.
Si francs estes, duz e gentiz,
Tutes terres vus sunt pais;
Si faus estes e surquidez,
520   Estranges estes u futes nez.
Ore vus dirrai un autre ren
Dunt vus me poez crere ben:
Ki ad la chose ke lui pleise,
524   En tutes terres vit a eise;
Le pais nen ad en sei
Fors grant joie e bone fei.
Si vus sentez mal u damage,
528   Ne le rettez fors a tun curage.
Fetes le ben e ben averez,
Si mal vulez, vus en beverez.
La chose dunt hoem plus se pleint,
532   Sachez le ben, en sei remeint;
U par feint quor u par folie
L'em recuilt mal u musardie.   253a
Ki fous est, il est estrange
536   E ja ne serrat sanz chalange.
Ki cointes est, sages e pruz,
Il ert par tut amé de tuz.
Por ceo fet par tut bon estre
540   Ki de saveir fet sun mestre.
Por ceo lessez le toen duleir,
Kar jo nel teng pas a saveir.'

LE VEILLARD

Le veuz hoem se dresce atant
544   Por la resun del jofne enfant

516 el m. *V*   523 kil li pl. *V*   542 tinc *V*

E dist: 'Beau fiz, le seint Espirit
Vus gart le cors en fet, en dit,
Kar ben me avez ore ensensé
548 En poi de hure de grant pensé.
Ore ne vus celerai nule ren
Por ceo ke vus mei dites si ben.
Ore entendez une aventure
552 Ke poet avenir e trop est dure,
Ceo est la dolur ke jo vus chant:
Ke jo morrai jofnes enfant,
E tost me serra acumplie
556 Tute la joie de ceste vie.
E ceo me serreit,' fet il, 'mult grant gref
E a joie tolir un grant meschef.'

L'ENFANT

L'enfant se dresce a icest mot
560 E al veil respundi tantost:
'Sire, de ceo ne mentez pas,
Kar ne vus serreit mie a gas
De issi nestre e tost morir
564 Ke plus n'en pussez vus joiir
De cest secle ki veent e fu,
Cum icil ki est chanu.
Mes sachez ben, keke vus pleise,
568 Tuz ceus del mund [n']unt pas eise,
Ne la meseise n'unt pas tuz:
Tel est desus ki ert desuz.
Issi turne la roe de Fortune
572 Ke tuz avum la lei commune,   253b
Les uns le ben, les uns le mal,
Le un amuntant e l'autre aval.
Si vus estes jofnes e pruz,
576 Vistes de cors e vigerus,
Nel serrez pas tuz jurz, ami;

545 le *not in* V   549 Ore vus ne c. V   557 grant *not in* V   560 respont V
562 Kar vus ne s. V   564 ioier V   565 vint V   568 O *begins again here*; ne
nount pas V   569 nen nount pas V   571 t. reo fortune OV   573 Les uns les
beaus O   574 e *not in* O

Turné vus ert le gui parti:
Malades serrez u dolerus
580 En aukun tens u en plusurs.
Dunc di jeo ben ke mult vus vaut
Jofne morir, quant ren ne vus faut,
Ke attendre la mesaventure
584 Ke passera tute mesure.
Dunc vudriez vus aver la mort,
Ceo serreit vostre greinnur cunfort.
Certes, meuz vaut lesser le gué
588 Ke folement estre bainné.
Ausi vaut meuz morir enfant
Ke mult vivere por estre dolent.
Un autre ren ben vus dirrai
592 U ja ren ne i mentirai:
Si vus ussez quanke vus plest
E en tute ta vie ne usset dehet,
Fet vus serreit un beau servise,
596 Si fussez mort en ceste guise.
Car la veillesce ne passeriez mie,
Ja tant ne fust duce ta vie.'

[LE VEILLARD]

'Dunc tenez vus veillesce a mal?'

[L'ENFANT]

600 L'enfant respund: 'Sire, nanal.
Mes les dolurs tanz i sunt,
Nes vus dirreit nul hoem del mund.
L'en le troeve en l'escripture
604 Ke cil ki en age gueres dure,
Ke il dechece en veillesce,
Tutes dolurs li frunt destresce.
Dunc di jo ben: mult fet bon estre

578 vus i ert *O*   582 ne *not in OV*   584 passa *O*   589 Ausi meuz vaut m. *OV*
590 dolaunt *O*   592 U ia ne ny m. *O*; U ia nen ni m. *V*   594 E *not in V*; ussez *OV*
597 passerez *O*; ni passirez *V*   598 la vie *OV*   601 tauntes *OV*   602 Ne vus
d. *OV*   606 Tante d. *V*; funt *OV*

608 Mort en joie e pres le nestre,
    Ke atendre cele grant dolur
    Dunt ore beivent mult li plusur.   253c
    Quant jofne moert ki ad Deu servi,
612 Assez est veil, sachez de fi.
    Destiné tant a l'enfant si fu
    De tost morir cum al chanu.'

LE VEILLARD

    'Beau fiz,' fet il, 'vus dites veir,
616 Ore mei metez en bon espeir
    De une chose ke vus demand:
    U seit arere u seit avant,
    Morir m'estoet a chef de tur,
620 Seit ceo en joie u en dolur,
    Mes ben tost avenir porra
    Ke ja hoem ne me ensevelira,
    Mes issi girra[i] tut en apert,
624 A tute ren tut descovert,
    Si serrunt mult genz irascu
    De la puur u del cors nu,
    E mei serreit trop lede affere
628 Si mun cors n'est tost mis en terre.
    Les oiseals mei depincerunt
    E les gros luus mei devurrunt,
    E les mastins tut ensement;
632 Ceo me serreit un gref turment.'

L'ENFANT

    'Sire,' fet cil, 'jo vus dirrai,
    Ja mun avis ne vus celerai:
    Si enseveli nen estes mie,
636 Nel tenez pas a grant folie.
    Cent mille seinz joie reçurent,

L'enfant *is beside l. 633*

608 en j. en p. *O*   612 Asez v. est *V*   613 si *not in V*   614 a ch. *V*
623 issi serra t. *V*   625 mute g. *V*   633 fet il *O*; iol *V*   637 C. m. cenz *O*

Ki unkes en terre enseveliz ne furent:
U il sunt neez u en feu ars,
640 U de urs mangez u de lebarz.
E si vus dirrai un autre ren,
Gardez ke vus i entendez ben:
Quant l'alme del cors s'en ert parti,
644 Ceo ert sanz faille le giu parti
De tute gent, ceo me est avis.
E u ke le cors en seit remis,
Ren ne sentira de nul affere
648 Plus ke une bleste prise de terre.   *253d*
Dunc di jeo ke li cors ne sent
Si il est en terre u il gist al vent.
Dunc nen ad ren ke vus despleise,
652 Si vostre alme est a eise.'

LE VEILLARD

Li veil respund: 'Ceo ert grant hunte
Ke tant de mei ne tendrunt cunte
Ke nul ne vout sei entremettre
656 De le men cors en terre mettre.'

L'ENFANT

'Sire,' fet cil, 'jo vus dirrai ben
Cum a prudome iceste ren.
Jo ai oi en muz lius dire,
660 E vus le dussez ben saver, sire,
Ke unkes enterrement de cors
Ne fu cuntrové sul por les mors,
Mes por les vifs, sachez di fi.
664 Kar quant le cors en fust porri,
Dunt freit as vifs destructiun
La puur e la grant corruptiun,

---

640 de lous m. *O*   641 d. de un a. *V*   642 atendez *O*; uus lentendez *V*   643 sen est p. *V*   646 E *not in V*; en *not in O*   647 Ren] Ben *OV*   649 di io bien ke *V*   650 u g. al v. *O*   652 seit a e. *V*   653 *another* veil *in right-hand margin V* 654 ne]il *V*   655 Ke nul ke v. *O*   662 le m. *V*   663 le v. *V*   664 en *not in O*   665 feit *O*; a v. *OV*   666 grant *not in O*

E la hidur de l'esgarder
668 Freit mult as vifs le quor arder;
Kar le penser e la puur
Lur freit al quor mult grant dolur,
Ke ja heité ne serreient,
672 E de assez la gent vivereient
Meins ke ne firent sa en arere.
Dunt dussent il, sachez, beau pere,
Plus sei pener de l'ensevelir
676 Ke vus ki en devez morir.
Quant Deu l'ad issi porveu,
M'est avis de poi estes esmeu.'

LE VEILLARD

'Beau fiz,' fet cil, 'ceo poet ben estre,
680 Jo le vus otrei, seez vus mestre.
Tut seit il dit en reprover
Ke en veille gent est li saver,
Jo di por veir ke mult plus sage
684 Est ta juvente ke mun veil age.
Le sanc est chaut e le quor leger,
Li sens i poet ben herberger.   254*a*
Jo teng le veil a nunsavant
688 Ke plus quide valer ke un tel enfant;
Ja n'eit tant oi ne tant veu
Ke il ne poet estre por sot tenu.
Ore, beau frere, vus dirrai plus:
692 Gardez ke vus ne seez cunfus
Des aventures ke tanz avenent
E ke les quors en doel meintenent
De ceus ki sunt ore cheitifs;
696 Assez unt morz e plus les vifs.

680 mettre

668 mult *not in* V; a v. OV 669 la penser V 673 ne *not in* OV; ke il f. V
677 Q. issi d. lad p. V 678 Mes de poy estes en mu O; Mut de poi est mou V
679 Leau f. O; fet cil *not in* V 680 le *not in* V 682 Ken en V 686 herbiger V
687 tinc V 688 un] unt V 689 Ia neit oi OV 690 il *not in* V; por *not in* OV
692 conclus O 693 taunt OV 694 le q. V 695 De c. ke sunt kore sunt ch.
O; De c. ki sunt ke or sunt ch. V 696 le v. V

Des morz avum parlee assez
E vus me avez en tut passez;
Ore parlerum, si il vus plerreit,
700 De ceus ke vivent en grant destreit,
En anguisse e en grant dolur
Ke lur avenent e nut e jur.'

L'ENFANT

L'enfant respunt: 'Tut a leisir
704 Dirrez, beau pere, vostre pleisir.'

LE VEILLARD

'Vostre merci,' fet li veillart,
'E jo le vus dirrai, si Deu me gart,
Sanz curuz e sanz vileinie,
708 Des aventures de ceste vie
Ke avenent ore chescun jur
E si nus mettent en grant tristur.
Issi voil comencer mun cunte,
712 Ki primes l'ad gueres ne munte,
Ke est iceo: ja est la lie
De tun sein cors grant maladie,
Ke tei tendra en grant langur
716 Tute ta vie sanz nul retur,
Si te serra e jur e nut
Dolur remis por tun dedut.
Beau fiz,' fet il, 'ceo est la summe,
720 Iceo seofre meint gentil home.
Ore mei dirrez cuntre cest mal,
Kar cist en est mult communal.'

Le veillard *is beside l. 705*

697 De m. *OV*   699 il *not in OV*   701 e *not in O*   702 auent *OV*; a. nut *V*
703 tust a leiser *V*   704 Dites *O*, Dirre *V*   706 le *not in O*   710 nus] vus *O*
712 E puis i uerrez quei amounte *V*   714 s. c. la m. *V*   715 uendra *V*   722 en
not in O

L'ENFANT

Li vaslet dit: 'Mult volunters.
724 Ore me escutez endementers: 254*b*
Maladie nen est pas hunte
Si ele vostre cors surmunte,
Einz est la volunté de Dé
728 Ke vus estes si flaelé.
Un autre ren vus en dirrai,
U ja ren ne i mentirai:
Sachez le vus ben sanz faille
732 Ke en terre, en mer u en bataille
Ne esproeve l'en mie sulement
L'enterin quor e le hardement:
Ne lerrai pas ke nel vus die,
736 L'em le esproeve en maladie,
Enz la langur u vus girrez
Tun leal quor esproverez;
Quant ne s'esmaie, s'il soefre mult,
740 Iteu quor ert vaillant par tut.
Car, beau pere, sachez de veir,
Si mal vus met enz nunpoeir,
Le un de vus en ert le mestre,
744 Ensemble ne porrez tuz jurs estre;
Si vus ne la venkés a estrus,
La maladie venquira vus,
Si serra forte la bataille;
748 Gardez ke quor ne vus faille.
Si vus desesperez de ren
E quor vus faille, sachez le ben,
Vencuz en serrez vus plus tost
752 En maladie u seit en ost.
Por ceo di jo ke leal quor
Ne s'esmaera a nul foer.

723 iuuencel O   730 i *not in* O   731 Sachiez les uus *V*   732 t. u en m. O*V*
733 Repreoue mi len s. O; len *not in V*   735 pas ke *not in V*; ke *not in* O   736 Len
repreoue O   737 la *not in V*   739 se maye sil s. O; sei maie si s. *V*   740 est *V*
745 a esturs O*V*   749 desperez *V*   752 E m. *V*

          Autant deit estre redutee
756   En bataille le cop de espee
          Cum la haschee de la fevre
          Quant vus fet trembler la levre,
          Car ausi tost perdrez la vie
760   En bataille cum en maladie.'

                    [LE VEILLARD]

          'Ben est veirs,' fet il, 'beau frere,
          M'est vis ke en iceste manere   254*c*
          Porrai meuz la langur suffrir
764   Par teu penser recuillir.
          Mes ore mei dites un autre chose
          Ke par mei vus serra desclose
          De un aventure ke vent adés,
768   Ke a mun quor tout mult la pes:
          Ceo ke gent ne mei portent fei,
          Einz unt grant suspeciun de mei
          E quident ke jeo seie de assez
772   Plus mauveis e mult plus surquidez
          Ke ne sui par aventure.
          Por ceo ne sevent nule mesure
          De mei empeirer u de mesdire,
776   Si serrad mun quor en grant martyre,
          E sur mei mettrunt mult grant folie,
          Ke deservi ne l'averai mie.'

                    L'ENFANT

          L'enfant respund: 'Vus dites veir.
780   Sire,' fet il, 'a mun espeir
          Porreit un fol por une pome
          Fere grant hunte a un produme
          E sun renun mult empeirer

---

757 Cum ia h.

755 rendute *O*   756 le *not in V*   757 Cum la h. *OV*; hachie *V*   759 auter
si t. *O*   764 E par t. *V*   769 Co est ke *V*   772 mult *not in O*   773 Ke ieo
ne su *OV*   775 ou desmedire *V*   777 mult *not in OV*   778 ne aueray *OV*

784 Si il ne li donast sun bon luer.
    Ore vus dirrai ceo ke jeo en sent,
    Kar mult se peinent male gent
    De mesdire en dous e en treis
788 Autant des bons cum de mauveis.
    Ne poet chaleir de lur renun,
    Quant ne pensez si de ben nun.
    Por ceo ne vus penez mie
792 De prendre a fes trop lur folie.
    N'est pas custume, sachez, beau sire,
    A sages homes de trop mesdire,
    Mes bonement amender dussent
796 Vostre trespas, si il le seussent.
    Si seint Pol mesdeist de vus,
    Vus devriez estre anguissus,
    U seint Augustin u seint Gregoire;
800 Mult dust trubler vostre memorie.   254*d*
    Mes n'est pas lur entendement
    De mesdire mult de la gent,
    Ne nul autre sage nel frad,
804 Kar de l'escrit apris ne l'ad.
    Quant des sages ne vent mie,
    Dunc di jo ben ke de folie
    Cuvent venir, sachez de fi,
808 Ceste chose ke jo vus di.
    A mesdire a fous affert,
    Car lur mauvesté le quert
    K'il ne sachent de autre ben dire,
812 Car lur ben ne i poet suffire.
    Cil ki n'ad nul ben en sei,
    Coment le ben dirreit de tei?
    En plet ne deit aver escut
816 Ki est pendable de tut en tut,
    E larun ne deit autre juger,
    Quant il del fet est parcener.

---

784 li *not in V*; sun *not in OV*   785 ieo *not in OV*   787 en d. u en t. *O*   788 de b. *V*
789 lur nun *O*   793 Ne pas *V*; beau *not in O*   794 de *not in OV*   798 deuerez
OV   799 austyn *OV*; gregorie *O*   800 memoire *OV*   801 ne pas *V*
803 s. le frad *O*   805 de s. *OV*; ne uout? mye *O*   807 sage de fi *V*
811 ne s. nul ben dire *OV*   812 i *not in OV*   814 dirra *V*   818 de f. *O*

E

Dunc pri jo ke nul ne tenge plet
820　De ceo ke mauveis u dit u fet,
Ben le sachez, ke ceo est lur dreit,
De mesdire, coment ke seit,
E tuz jurs frunt mauveis record,
824　U seit a dreit u seit a tort.
De ceo quident fere bon plet,
Si de lur proeme dient le let.
Il quident estre tenuz plus cher,
828　Si par mal poent autre empeirer.
Empeirer gueres ne porrunt mie,
Tut dient il lur grant folie;
Tost aparceverunt sage gent
832　Lur mauvesté apertement,
Car ja ben dire ne porrunt,
Por ceo ke en custume ne l'unt.
Ore les lessez fere, beau pere,
836　Ceo k'il unt usee sa en arere,
Car de escufle u de busard
Bon ostur averez vus mult tart.　　　　　255a
A sages vus acumpaignez,
840　Vus ne i perdrez, si ne i gainnez;
En pes serra vostre curage
En cumpaignie de home sage;
E si les fous vulez crere,
844　Ja nen averez vus pes en terre.
Jo lou ke vus ne mettez mie
Tun sen cuntre lur folie,
Car si il ne mesdeissent de tei,
848　De autre le freient, si cum jo crei.
Ennuuse lange e mauveise,
Quant ne mesdit, n'est pas a eise.'

LE VEILLARD

'Beau fiz,' respunt dunc li veillart,

820 ke m. d. OV　　　　821 ke] kar V, k O　　　　823 funt OV　　　　826 del lur V
834 K coe V　　　　838 mult *not in* O　　　　840 ni perdez ren si O; perdez si en g. V
844 Ia nen nauerez pes O; Ia ne auerez pes V　　　846 encuntre O　　　847 mesdient OV
849 Enuyuse OV　　　850 Q. ele ne m. O; mefet V　　　851 dunc *not in* O

852 'Ben dites veir, si Deu me gart,
    N'ad home ke seit u eit esté
    Ki peust estuper lur mauvesté.
    Dunc lou jo ben, sanz repentir,
856 Ke nus les lessum a cunvenir.
    Mes, beau fiz, sachez le vus,
    De un autre ren sui anguissus,
    Ke jo sui sanz ma deserte
860 Ore cheet en grant poverte.
    De tutes parz mei curent sure
    Pleintes, dolurs e mesaventure,
    Defautes, feim e sei e freit,
864 Une de ses trubler mei deit.
    E mult me greve, sachez, sanz fin,
    Ke tant sunt riches tut mi veisin.
    Or e argent unt il assez
868 E trestutes lur voluntez,
    Fors jo ki sui sul meseisee:
    Mar vint le hure ke jo fui né.'

L'ENFANT

    L'enfant respund: 'Merci, beau sire.
872 Ceo ne vodrei pas ore oir dire
    Ke vus maudissez ta vie   255b
    Por nule empeinte de folie.
    Deskes ore me avez ben entendu,
876 E jo te ai aukes ben defendu
    De doleir por nule aventure,
    E ke od vus eussez sen e mesure.
    Uncore dirreie ci endreit
880 Mun avis, cument ke seit,
    Si a vus ne annue ma resun.'

[LE VEILLARD]

    'Ne place a Deu,' fet li prudum,

854 poet O   856 Ke nus lessum cil a. OV   859 io *not in* O   860 chew V
862 e *not in* V   864 ses] ces O, ceus V   870 fu ieo O   871 b. pere O
872 oyr ne dire O   878 ussessez O   879 dirrei. e ci e. O; dirrei e ci e. V   881 Sa
a uus namye O; Sire ne ws plest mie ma r. V   882 a *not in* V

'Mes mult me set e mult me plest.'

[L'ENFANT]

884 L'enfant respund e cil se test:
'Sire,' fet cil, 'par mun chef,
Jo vus dirrai cuntre cest gref:
Poverte ke vus tant blamez,

888 Vus mesfetes si ne l'amez,
Car primes vus fist ele cumpaignie,
Quant entrastes en ceste vie.
Ren ne i portastes si lui nun,

892 Ele fu tute ta possessiun,
Ne n'aviez mie tant de gages
Dunt pussez vus coverir les nages.
Por ceo la dussez mult amer

896 E mult cherir e honorer.
Deu, quant en terre cunversa,
Mult la honora e preisa.
Mult preisez ore Deu petit,

900 Quant vus tenez si en despit
La chose k'il plus amat en terre,
Quant il vint les seinz cunquerre.
Seure chose ad en poverte,

904 Hoem ne i avera dolur ne perte.
Si freit avez u sei u feim,
Trop ne en pensez cuntre demein,
Car icil ki vus furma

908 Assez tost vus pestera.   255c
Ore me dirrez cum ciw u borne:
Issi me dune Deu boef par la corne.
Vus mesquidez. Savez por quei?

912 Si nel savez, jo le vus dirrai:
Deu nule creature ne fist
Ke vitaille ne li porveist.

909 dirreit

885 fet il O   886 co gref V   888 me fetez sil ne a. V   893 Nen nauiez O,
Ne auiez V   894 vus *not in* O   895 d. plus amer OV   896 anurer O
898 Mut la p. e h. OV   901 kil ama plus V   906 en *not in* V   909 dirrez
not in O   910 doine V   912 Si vus uulez O

Autrement porreit chescun dire
916 Ke Deu l'ust fet por lui oscire
De feim u de freit u autrement;
Ne place a Deu omnipotent.
Ben li porveit sa poture
920 Deu, quant fet sa creature,
Car en wrec ne larrad mie,
Quant l'ad mis en ceste vie.
As bestes pert e as oiseals volanz
924 E en la mer as peissuns nuanz,
Car quant le jur apert tut cler,
Ne sevent pas de quei disner.
Car cum einz dis, lur porverrat
928 Icil Deu ki fet les ad,
Si ert chescune creature
E beauz e runz en sa nature.
Mes vus, ki dussez guverner
932 Quanke vit en terre e en mer
Desuz Deu, por lui servir,
Vus memes ne savez meintenir.
Quant plenté averunt tute ren,
936 Dunc n'averez vus gueres de ben.
Savez por quei? Jo le vus dirrai
E en escrit le vus troverai:
Quant vus en estes trop curius,
940 Deus em pensera le meins de vus.
Vus quidez ke vostre porveance
Plus vaille ke Deu e sa pussance;
Por ceo en avez fautes le plus   255d
944 Ke desesperez de Deu la sus.
Poverte est en sei mult fine
E si est nette e enterrine.
Si por lui estes anguissus,
948 Ele est mult plus encumbré de vus,
Car de tun quor avendrat

944 Ki

915 purra *V*   916 lui *not in V*   917 De f. u f. *O*; De f. de f. *V*   918 a *not in O V*
919 sa pouerte *O*, poesture *V*   920 Deu cuntrefet *O*   923 A b. pest e a o. *V*
924 E *not in V*   926 pas difiner *V*   929 Seit ch. *V*   938 le *not in V*
944 desperez *O V*   946 aterryne *O*   947 E pur *V*

La mauvesté, si nule i ad.
Si de pleindre ne vus poez tenir,
952 Car ceo porra ben avenir,
Ne poet chaleir fors ke ne pusse
Ta pleinte descoverir por nul anguisse
La priveté de vostre curage.
956 Dunt vus tendrai jo a ben sage,
Car reisun deit en tute manere
Veintre dolur e mettre arere.'

L'ENFANT

'Beau pere, unkore vus dirrai plus,
960 Ke vus ne seez del tut cunfus:
Si tun veisin est ja trop riche,
Il est fous large u il est chiche.
Si il est chice e trop aver,
964 Ja pru n'avera de sun aver,
Car endurer ne porra mie
Ren despendre por sa vie,
Mes amasser tuz jurs tresors
968 A autrui oes, quant serra mors.
Dunc di jo ke sa richesce bele
Ne li vaut pas une cenele.
Si il seit foularge e eit assez,
972 Gueres ne li dorra, ben le sachez,
Mes tost irra en declin
La richesce de tun veisin.
Li riches est, sachez de fi,
976 Plus dolurus e plus mari
Sovent ke li povre ne seit.
Car, seit a tort u seit a dreit,   256a
Bailifs, viscuntes e wandelarz
980 Li pincerunt de tutes parz
E encheisun li porquerrunt
De li tolir ceo k'il porrunt.

957 deit ben en t. O   960 nel seez O   962 chinche V   963 chinche V
966 Ben d. ne porra mye O; Ken en d. V   971 Si il est OV   977 pore V
978 u *not in* O   981 E *not in* V; purquerent O   982 co ki p. V

Quant li povres s'en vet juer,
984 Cuveent al riche plegges trover,
Si ert li riche plus travillee
Par tut en plez e en cuntee.
Issi avera le riche le quor amer
988 Par encheisun de sun aver;
Beivre e manger li toudra
E por pensers ne dormira,
Si avera por defendre l'aver
992 Gran amertume e grant penser.
Issi encurra ben maladie
U, poet cel estre, perdre la vie.
Dunc di jeo ben ke povere en joie
996 Vau meuz ke riche en te[le] voie.'

LE VEILLARD

Li veil respund: 'Veir avez dit,
Mes ore mei dites un petit:
Si jo ai eu sa en arere
1000 Joie grant en meinte manere
De ma richesce, mes par grant perte
Sui devenu en teu poverte,
E le record me ert mult gref
1004 De ma grant eise e de mun meschef.'

L'ENFANT

L'enfant respund: 'Certes, beau sire,
De assez porriez vus meuz dire
Ke Fortune te ad deschargee
1008 De un fes ke ele vus out trop surchargé.
Savez coment?' 'Beau fiz, nenal!'
'Jo le vus dirrai,' fet il, 'sanz mal:
Richesce de vus est departie

L'enfant *is beside l. 1005*

983 sen fet *V*   984 a r. *O*   996 tele v. *OV*   998 me d. uus un
p. *OV*   1000 Ioye en mute m. *O*; Ioie en hu en m. m. *V*   1008 f. kil, charge *O*
1009 Saueuz *O*   1011 partye *O*

1012   E mult ad fet grant curteisie   256b
        Ke hunie ne vus ad ne ledengee:
        De tant s'en est vers vus changee
        Plus ke vers nul autre hume.

1016   Car au derein ert ceo la summe:
        Ele perdera le hume u le hume li,
        Car le un des dous ert maubailli.
        Ja ne vus celerai,' fet il, 'beau pere,

1020   Hoem veint richesce en teu manere
        Quant il ne quert ren fors assez
        De ceo k'il avera tant amassez:
        Ceo est beivre, manger e vestir

1024   Od grant mesure, por Deu servir,
        E del surplus a bone gent
        Face aumoines e ben suvent,
        Ne mie murdrir en sun tresor

1028   Cofres pleines de argent u de or.
        Cist veint richesce par grant reisun,
        Car il n'e[n] tent plet si poi nun.
        Mes l'autre manere est trop dure,

1032   Quant richesce met le hume en cure.
        Issi le veint; savez cument?
        Ore vus dirrai tut erraument:
        Quant hoem se peine de sun tresor

1036   Por amasser argent e or
        E ne vout de ceo ben fere,
        Ceo est un langur ki est en terre.
        Car sul nel porra pas tut user

1040   En vesture ne en chaucer,
        E beiv[r]e e manger ne porra mie
        Plus de un autre en ceste vie.
        E le surplus u devendra,

1044   Quant il ne autre pas ne l'avera?
        A chef de tur, sachez de veir,
        Le venquira icest aveir;   256c

1013 Ke hume ne vus ad l. O; Ke home ne uus nad lendenge V   1016 au d. ceo
ert O   1018 de d. OV   1019 fet il not in V   1020 H. veit r. V   1023 e le
v. V   1028 a. e de or V   1029 Cist v. riche OV   1030 il ne t. V
1032 le not in O   1039 ne p. V   1041 En b. en m. O; A b. en m. V   1044 pas
not in O   1045 pur v. OV   1046 Len v. O

Estranges en frunt lur volunté
1048 E il en serra tuz jurs dampné.
Dunc di ke ben te est avenu,
Quant cest aver avez perdu.
Si cuveitise en fust partie
1052 Od tut le aveir de ceste vie,
Sachez le vus, par ceste perte
Benuree serriez en ta poverte.
E si entendez un autre ren
1056 Ke jo vus dirrai ja mult ben:
Si perdue avez ta richesce
U par fortune u par destresce,
Ne devez par reisun ren doleir,
1060 Car trestut le vostre aveir
Perdi autrui e plus assez
Devant ceo ke vus unkes l'ussez.
De autrui futes joius e lez
1064 E de autrui estes si adulez.
Ceo semble ben ke ceo seit volage,
As fous affert, ne mie a sage.
Meuz vaut perdre por estre seur
1068 Ke aver de perte tuz jurs pour.'

LE VEILLARD

Li veillart dunt li respundi:
'Beau fiz,' fet il, 'ben le vus di
Ke ben me avez assuagee
1072 En icest cas de mun pensee.
Ore vus dirrai un record
Ki me fet de dreit le tort,
Car mult me greve le damage
1076 E mult mei truble le curage.
Quel ke ceo seit, sen u folie,
Ja m'estoet ke jo le vus die.

1059 pas reisun

1047 en] i O   1048 Cil en s. OV   1049 di ieo ke O, di bien ke V   1051 len f.
O; sen f. V   1054 serrez OV   1056 jo *not in* OV ····1058 U par force OV
1062 unkes *not in* O   1064 si *not in* O   1065 ke seit v. OV   1066 A f. OV
1078 mestut V

Jo ai par mesaventure
1080 Tute perdue ma engendrure, *256d*
Kar mors sunt sudeinement
Mes enfanz, dunt sui dolent.
Ja ne recoverai iceste perte;
1084 Plus est dure ke poverte,
Car la richesce de cest munde
Vers mun enfant ren ne amunte.'

L'ENFANT

Li prudum atant se tut,
1088 E l'enfant la teste mut
Vers le prudum e dist en haut:
'Sire,' fet il, 'si Deu me saut,
De tute vostre aventure
1092 Ceste resemble la plus dure.
Por ceo le me avez tant celee
Ke avant ne l'as nomee.'

LE VEILLARD

'Ben est veir,' fet li veillart,
1096 'Car ceo fu la meillure part
Ke pesa aveie porveu,
E u tute ma fiance fu,
Ke jo usse greinnur cunfort
1100 E remembrance, quant fusse mort.
Car mun eir estre devreit
De quanke jo oi gainné par dreit.
Ore est mors a chef de tur;
1104 De [ceo] en ai si grant dolur.'

L'ENFANT

'Ben poet estre,' fet dunc l'enfant;
'Ore enquerrum de cest avant.

L'enfant *is beside l. 1087*

1085 ceo *V*; mund *OV*   1086 ne munte *O*; amount *V*   1087 Si p. *O*   1093 le *not in O*; Pur ceo mauez le itant c. *V*   1095 Len *O, but* L *erased*   1098 E *not in V* 1100 En r. *O*   1101 Ki *V*   1102 io ai g. *V*   1104 De ceo en ay mut g. d. *OV* 1106 aquerrum *V*

Vus mei semblez, sire, par Dé,
1108 Cum un pomer ki est chargé,
Ki se brise tut a scient
Por une pome ki chet al vent.
Si fetes vus, quant sanz cunfort
1112 Pleinnez de un enfant la mort.
Folie est e grant ennui
Mortel pleindre de mor d'autrui.   257a
Quant cil s'en vet memes la voie,
1116 Il pleint celui ki le cunvoie.
N'est pas sul en icest cas,
Les hauz i sunt, si sunt les bas.
Sachez, en terre n'ad si haut reis
1120 Ne duc ne cunte ki eit paleis,
Ke acune feiz ne se pleine
De ceste perte, kek'il en gainne.
Car si tost pert le rei sun fiz
1124 Cum fet celui ki est mendifs,
E si en ad greinnur mester
Ke n'averad un pautener
Ki ben averad u set u ut
1128 Porchacee par sun dedut.
Mes al re cuvent por veir
Sun barnage garnir par eir.
Si il nel fet, creez en mei,
1132 Le reaume irrad a besley,
Car a chescun sun quor dune
Ke il enporte la corune.
Si le reis pert issi sun eir,
1136 Dunc en poet un doel aveir,
Ne mie por sei, mes por sa gent
Ki se demenerunt malement.
Quant il en ert de ci parti,
1140 Li meins pussant ert fors parti.
Mes vus ki estes un paisant

1109 bruse O   1110 a v. V   1114 p. de la mort O; p. la m. V   1115 sen
not in O   1116 Si pl. O   1117 Nestes pas OV   1118 Les h. i sunt e li b. O
1119 ni ad O   1122 ceste part O   1124 fet *not in* OV   1126 Ke nen a. O, Ken
nauera V   1127 bien a. seet V   1128 Par cas e V   1131 ne fet V   1137 pur
sei meimes me V   1138 si demeorent O; demerrunt V   1140 forparti O

E si n'avez fors un enfant,
E cil vus est mort sanz faille,
1144 De ceo fetes si grant bataille
Ke ne vulez aver cunfort.
Beau duz sire, vus avez tort,
Car vus ne savez a chef de tur
1148 Si il ert sages u hasardur,
E quant il ne vus verra,
Dunc frad iceo ke lui plerra.
Meuz vaut, si il n'ad nul sens,   *257b*
1152 Ke vostre eir moerge par tens,
Car vus serriez tute sa vie
Suvent dolent por sa folie.
Ore vus dirrai, beau sire, aprés,
1156 Por meuz sauver la vostre pes,
Fu ceo en vus demeintenant
Quant vuliez, de engendrer enfant?'

LE VEILLARD

'Nenal,' fet li veillart, 'beau frere.'

L'ENFANT

1160 'En ki dunc,' fet il, 'beau pere?'

LE VEILLARD

'Ceo est en Deu, le tut pussant,
Ki me grante de aver enfant.'

L'ENFANT

'Vus dites veir,' fet il, 'par fei;
1164 Ore vus dirrai ceo ke jo i vei:
Si Deu vus dune,' fet il, 'enfant

Le veillard *is beside l. 1159*, L'enfant *beside l. 1160*, Le veillard *beside l. 1161*

1152 murge *V*   1156 sauer *O*   1158 de gu gendrer *V*   1162 graunt *O*;
granta *V*   1164 i *not in* O*V*

Por vus dedure ben en avant,
Si il le vus toust a chef de tur,
1168 Ne devez trop fere dolur,
Si ne vulez par mauvesté
Desdire Deu e sa volunté.
Cungé ne vus deit demander
1172 Plus al tolir ke al duner.
Ne dolez pas, si fras ke sage;
Ceo ke Deu fet n'est pas utrage.'

LE VEILLARD

'Ben poet estre,' fet li veillart,
1176 'Mes ore mei dites, si Dé vus gard,
De un aventure ke trop mei greve
E ma dolur james n'i cheve,
Ceo est la greinnur dolur del mund
1180 Ke plus me greve e plus cunfund.
E ben est dreit ke jo le vus die
Ke jo ai perdue ma duce amie
Ke ma leale espuse esteit;
1184 De ceo doler en ai grant dreit.
Ceo fu la plus duce ke fust
E la plus franche ke l'en seust.
Leale fu mult e enterrine,
1188 De beauté passa la flur d'espine.   257c
De tuz bens, keke l'en die,
Aveit ele mult grant partie,
E tutes femmes passa ele,
1192 Si cum saphir fet la gravele.
Por ceo la amai tant cum jo faz,
Car ele fu mun greinnur solaz.
Ore est morte, si m'ad lessee,
1196 Dunt ma joie est tute aquassé,
E si ne pus en nule voie
Dedenz mun quor recuillir joie.

1171 Quoynge O   1172 a t. V   1173 frez OV   1174 ne pas V   1175 Len O, *with* L *erased*   1178 i *not in* OV; chive V   1180 e plus me c. O   1181 le *not in* O   1184 en ad g. d. V   1187 e *not in* V   1192 Si cum le s. O   1195 est *not in* V   1196 dequasse O   1197 E si ieo ne pus OV

Plus tost morrai, ceo me est vis,
1200 Ke aprés lui fusse un tel cheitifs.
Mes, beau fiz, sachez, sanz li
De quor serrai mult maubailli.
Ore me devez mult solacer,
1204 Car jo en ai mult grant mester.'

L'ENFANT

'Certes, ceo est veir,' fet dunc l'enfant,
'Ci en avez mester mult grant
De beau solaz e de cunfort,
1208 Car jo sai ben ke ceste mort
Perce tun quor mult plus de assez
Ke ceo ke tut as amassez
De aventures sa en arere.
1212 Ore me entendez,' fet il, 'beau pere:
Quant tant pleinnez vostre amie,
N'est pas merveille, si fous se i fie;
Si ele fu sage, bele e curteise,
1216 Bone serreit, si ne deveneist maveise.
N'ad suz cel home ki seit vivant
Ke ele ne deceive par beau semblant.
Ele vus fet de feble fort,
1220 Ele vus fet de dreit le tort,
Ele vus fet de freit le chaut,
Ele vus fet de bas le haut,
Ele vus fet de blanc le neir,
1224 De la folie vus fra le saveir.
Quanke vulez, fra le cuntraire   257d
Femme, quant serra demaleire.
Quant vus acole vostre amie,
1228 Dunc vus gardez de felunie.
N'ad femme ke seit desuz la nue,
Ke jofne seit u seit chanue,

1199 avis *OV*   1201 Mun b. f. *OV*   1203 Ore men d. *OV*   1205 dunc *not in O*
1209 plus ke a. *O*   1210 ke tu as a. *V*   1212 atendez *O*   1214 Ne pas *V*; i *not
in V*   1215 fust *O*   1216 Donc s. si ele d. *V*   1217 ki seit *not in O*; de femes *in
right-hand margin V*   1218 ele *not in OV*   1229 sur la nue *OV*   1230 j. seit u
ch. *O*

Si ele vus vout gueres grever,
1232　Ke ele ne vus face mal achever.
Tant sevent eles wanelaces,
Ki ben lur fet, poi en ad graces.
Si ele vus vout u mal u ben,
1236　Semblant ne fra de nule ren.
Dunc la creez et seet cert,
Quant felunesse vus ert en apert.
Ne di pas ke tutes teles seient,
1240　Nent plus ke ceus ki me diseient
Ke le lu resemblout le chen.
Ore me poez crere mult ben,
Ne sunt pas tutes si demaleires,
1244　Mutes en sunt mult deboneires,
E Deus en cresse tost lur numbre
Ke la fausime ne les encumbre.
Mult en serreie joius e lee,
1248　Si jo susse ore de veritee
Si mutes fussent de tel affere
Dunt jo vei aukunes en terre,
De bunté pleines e de franchise,
1252　De naturesce e de bele aprise,
E grant leauté unt eles en sei,
Ceo vus pus jo affier, par fei.
E mar en seit nul en dutance,
1256　En Engletere sunt plus ke en France.
Nekedent par tut luist la lune,
En France poet l'en aver aucune.
Chescune terre, coment ke seit,
1260　Ke aucun ben eit, est reisun e dreit.
Mes de celes en est flurie
Engletere cum bele praerie.　　　　258a
Tuz les reames ke ore sunt
1264　Passe Engletere, e savez dunt?

1240 Nept

1233 wenelaces O, wenlaces V　　1234 lur *not in* OV; Ke bien en fet V　　1238 en
not in O; uie *inserted above line after* felunesse V　　1244 mult *not in* O　　1245 e. tut
lur n. O　　1248 ore la v. V　　1257 lut O　　1258 En fr. en poet aver OV
1259 terre *not in* OV　　1260 r. de dr. OV　　1261 teles OV

De tuz deduz e de franchise.
Si femmes i sunt de bele aprise,
Ne devez pas esmerveiller,
1268   Si sunt assez li chevaler,
E tuz li autre ki sunt aprés
Sunt pruz, gentils e francs adés,
Fors sul itant ke beverie
1272   Empire mult lur bele vie.
Mes tu as ore perdu ta drue,
Ben est chose aparceue,
E vus l'avez de mult preisee:
1276   Leale fu, bele e enveisee.
Ore sai jeo ben par vostre dit
Ke vus l'amastes de grant affit.
Por ceo dist li Engleis trop ben:
1280   Tant cum l'amez, luez tun chen
E ta femme e tun cheval.
Kek'il i eit, u ben u mal,
Amur prise e met en haut
1284   Chescune ren plus k'ele ne vaut.'

LE VEILLARD

Li prudum dist tut a estrus:
'Mun beau duz fiz, sachez le vus,
Ke tant sui seur e tant hardi
1288   E de sa leauté itant me fi
Ke unkes tecche de folie
N'out ne n'avereit ma duce amie.'

L'ENFANT

L'enfant respund: 'Tut seurement,
1292   Ceo poez dire ore hardiement,

1268 chevalez   1282 Keke li eit   Le veillard *is beside l. 1285,* L'enfant *beside l. 1289*

1267 ameruiller *O*, en meruiller *V*   1278 vus amyez *O*; lamiez *V*   1280 luez]
liez *V*; cum ch. *O*   1281 E ta f. cum ch. *O*   1282 eit] ert *V*; eyt b. u m. *O*
1284 E ch. ren plus ke ne v. *O*   1288 men fi *V*   1290 Ne nout ne nauereit *O*; Ne
uout ne neuerreit *V*   1292 peot *O*

Car la mort, si cum jo quit,
Vus ad averee vostre dit.
Si ele fu franche e deboneire,
1296 La mort li ad recopé sun eire   258*b*
Ke ele ne changast sun quor avant,
Cum feverer tredze covenant.
Femme resemble flur de engleter
1300 E si se tent cum vent en mer,
Ore est al west, ore est en le est,
Quant plus jangleie, tantost se test.
N'ad desuz la chape del cel
1304 Ren ke se moet u seit mortel,
Ke tant se change e pres e loin,
Cum quor de femme, quant ad busoin.
Si femme sent u ben u mal,
1308 Ore est la sus, ore est la val,
Ore est dedenz, ore est dehors;
U n'ert li quor, si ert li cors.'

LE VEILLARD

'Certes, beau fiz, ceo est ben veir,
1312 Mes vus ne entendez mun espeir
Ke perdu ai ma leale amie,
Ke fu ma joie en ceste vie,
E vus me deistes sa en arere:
1316 Ne sunt pas tutes de une manere.
Les unes sunt bones sanz faille,
Les unes ne valent une maille,
E les mauveises tant en funt
1320 Ke les bones crewes ne sunt.
Mes jo sai ben, keke l'em die,
Ke tutes passe la meie amie
De tuz bens e de bones murs,
1324 E en ceo se tendreit ele tuz jurs,

1294 ad *not in* O   1296 coupe O   1298 tresze O, treze V   1299 eglenter
O, englenter V   1301 en le w. O, el w. V   1302 changle V   1304 Ren
ke se mort ke seyt m. O; Rien que seit meur V   1310 U nout li q. si est li c. V
1312 nentendez pas OV   1313 p. ad V; ma bele amie OV   1318 vaillent V
1320 creues V   1322 passa V   1323 bons m. OV   1324 ele *not in* OV

F

Car l'aprise out en juvente,
E ele i aveit mult mis sa entente.
E ke aprent pulein en danture,
1328 L'em dist ke lung tens li dure.
Mes ma amie aveit de Deu dun
De tutes grace[s] a grant fuisun,   258c
Tut ne l'eust ele de aprise,
1332 Car ele valut meuz en sa chemise
Ke tutes celes ke sunt al munde,
Ki les cerchast a la runde.
Car ausi seur fu jo de li
1336 Cum de mei memes, sachez de fi.
Ore est morte e trop me doil,
E plus sui murnes ke jo ne soil.'

L'ENFANT

'Ore oi merveilles,' fet dunc l'enfant,
1340 'Ke vus alez si dolusant
Por vostre amie ke leale fu.
Si vus mei ussez ben entendu,
Vus lerriez cele dolur.
1344 Aveit ele unkes si grant amur
Vers vus, cum vus aviez vers li?'

LE VEILLARD

'Oil, e assez plus, sachez de fi.'

L'ENFANT

'Par fei, ceo est merveille grant,
1348 Car mes ne oi en mun vivant,
Ben le vus di, mun beau pere,

Le veillard *is beside l. 1346*, L'enfant *beside l. 1347*

1325 Ki *V*   1326 Cele *O*   1329 aveit] out *O*   1330 graces f. *O*; graces a
f. *V* 1331 de prise *O*   1332 vaut *O*   1333 el m. *OV*   1337 men doil *V*
1339 dunc *not in O*   1342 mei *not in OV*   1343 cel d. *V*   1344 Aueyt unkes
ele *O*   1345 auez *V*   1348 a mun v. *V*   1349 mun *not in O*

Ke femme eust iteu manere
Ke femme amast, quant fud amee.
1352 Mes oez lur dreite destinee:
Si ele se aparceit ke l'em la eime,
Dunc por hunie ben se cleime,
Si tost ne devenge dangeruse
1356 U mult enrevere e trop irruse.
Si ren dites cuntre sun voil,
Ele vus regardera de l'autre oil.
Mes celui ki ne la eime de ren,
1360 A celui juera ele ben
E acolera e suef beisera
E par beal semblant ben le atrerra.
Mes de celui dunt est seure,
1364 Sachez, ne en prendra gueres cure.   258d
Chescune femme devant l'espusaille
Mult beal semblant vus fra sanz faille.
Quant ele vus dist: "Seez certein,
1368 Mun tresduz quor, car trop vus eim,"
Dunc dist sun quor: "Vus i mentez;
Tut autrement cherrunt les dez.
Fous se fie en mun semblant,
1372 Mun quor ne i est ne tant ne quant.
Ki de mun semblant mult se lue,
Cil tent l'anguille dreit par la cue."
Mun beau pere, sachez de fi,
1376 Ja nul hoem ki unkes nasqui
Ne vit ren ke tant seit volage
Cum est femme e[n] sun curage.
Coment porriez dunc aseurer
1380 En ta amie e tant jurer
Ke jamés ne se changereit

1366 frai

1350 de iteu m. *V*   1351 *not in* O   1352 dreyt d. O   1353 Si ele parceyt O*V*
1356 areure O, enriuere *V*; u trop i. O*V*   1357 encuntre O   1362 trera O
1365 femme *not in* O*V*   1368 car] ke O   1369 vus i mettrez O   1371 en lur
s. *V*   1372 Mun ni est taunt ne q. O; Lur semblant ne vaut t. ne q. *V*   1373 de
lur s. *V*   1374 l' *not in* O   1375 dount seez certeyne sachez de fi *in right-hand
margin V*   1379-80 *reversed in* O*V*   1379 assenter O*V*   1380 ostant j. *V*

Deske a la mort, coment ke seit?
Mes jo, ki su jofne enfant,
1384 Ore vus dirrai merveille grant:
Mult ai oi, sachez, beau pere,
Femmes changer sa en arere.
Jo ai veu chaste espuse e leale
1388 En poi de ure devenir cursale,
E tele ke de dulçur n'aveit per
Mult felunesse au paraler,
E mult simple, duce e coye
1392 Mettre sun dru en male voie.
Les plus devorz ke unt esté
Firent femmes par mauvesté.
Si ren i ad ke lur desplet,
1396 Enz en chapitres moevent lur plet.
L'une dist ke le soen mari
Est lere fort, si n'est par li.   259a
L'autre dist ke le soen est un chevre,
1400 L'espus a l'autre est felun e enrevre.
Icele dist ke ele ad grant dreit
Ke cil ne li fet ke fere deit.
Issi se peine por un curuz
1404 Chescune hunir sun ami duz.
Ben quide chescune ke ben se avance,
Si porchaser poet la deseverance;
Si nun, mult se tendra hunie,
1408 Ne il n'avera pes jur de sa vie.
Unc n'i vi femme itant amer
Ne tant cherir sun bacheler,
Si ele veist un plus beals de li,
1412 Ke ele nel coveitast, sachez de fi.
Vent u fumee u nyule en mer
Est quor de femme, quant vout amer.'

1382 *At foot of V fol. 96b* Vent ou fumee ou nille en mer/est quor de femme quan
vult amer (= 1413–14)   1385 sachez *not in* O   1388 venir *V*   1389 per] espeir
with s *and* i *expuncted V*   1392 a m. v. *V*   1394 Furent O   1395 mesplet O*V*
1399 kil s. est ch. O; est chivere *V*   1400 Le espus lautre O; rivere *V*   1401 mut
grant d. *V*   1405 ke mut sauance OV   1408 Nel nauera *V*   1409 i *not in* OV
1411 veit *V*

LE VEILLARD

'Beau fiz, merci,' fet li prudum,
1416 'Por Deu e sun seintisme nun
Temprez tun dit e tun curage
Ke ne lur diez si grant utrage.
"Ne tut dire ne tut lesser,"
1420 Dist li sages en reprover.
Jo ai perdue ma duce amie,
Ke mult mei greve, keke l'em die,
E la perte ert sanz recoverer,
1424 Car jo n'averai jamés sa per.'

L'ENFANT

'Sire,' fet cil, 'mult volunters
Pes lur durrai endementers.
Por vostre amur, queke il i eit,
1428 Desoremés parduné seit.
E neporoek muz acheisuns,
Ke por vostre amur lerruns,
I avereit aprés, sacher de veir,
1432 Por vus tolir vostre doleir.   259*b*
Mes ore mei dites e repruvez
Ke jamés tele nen averez.
Querez la, si l'averez ben,
1436 Si vus ne demandez autre ren
Fors itele cum cele fu.
E ausi jofne cum jeo su
Vus aprendrai mult ben coment
1440 La choiserez, si jo ne ment:
Regardez l'aprise e la porture,
Sa gentrise e sa mesure.
Beau sire, ne regardez mie
1444 Ke plusurs avoegle en cest[e] vie,

Le veillard *is beside l. 1415*   1437 celu

1415 fet] fe *O*   1427 q. illi eit *V*   1429 E nequedent *V*; enchesuns *OV*
1431 Il verreit a. sachez de uenir *O*; I uerreit, sachiez *V*   1433 en reprouerz *O*;
en r. *V*   1437 cele fu *OV*   1438 autre si *O*

Ceo sunt les terres e les tresors;
Mes si un regardast ben le cors,
Por nul aveir, coment ke seit,
1448 A femme, sachez, ne la prendreit;
Car quant le aveir ert avalee,
Al mal ert li cheitif alee.
Richesce irra a chef de tur
1452 E cil se tendra a la dolur,
Car le chatel si fu visere
Ke ne fu coneue sa manere.
Mes si ele est bele e afeitee,
1456 Tut seit ele de povres nee,
Plus seur serrer de vostre amie,
De sun aport ne se orgoillera mie.
Si vus volez femme prendre,
1460 Tele adevent ke vus frad despendre
Plus ke vostre rente gueres ne amunte,
Ceo vus serreit un vilein cunte.
Quant vus averez femme espusee,
1464 E vers ta mesun en ert menee,
Plus vaudra sa robe e sun herneis
Ke ta rente dous anz u treis,   259c
E ses juaus e sun argent
1468 U vus ne ficherez ja le dent.
Ele vus repruvera mult ben:
"Cest ert e fu, sire, le men.
De mes amis vint ceste proie,
1472 Dunt jo demein issi grant joie.
Si vus ne me tengez issi avant,
Jo vus en faz le covenant
Ke jo me pleindrai a mes amis
1476 Ki vus frunt de mal le pis."
Si serrad en iceste guise
Vostre grant pes mult entreprise.
Ore seit issi ke si avenge

1449 est *V*   1450 A mal *O*   1451 au c. de t. *O*   1453 ch. li fui *OV*   1454 fu
not in O   1455 est *not in* O*V*; e feytee *O*   1457 serrez *OV*   1459 Si vus deuez *O*
1460 auent *O*   1461 gueres *not in O*   1464 en *not in OV*   1467 E ces j. *O*
1468 la d. *OV*   1470 ert e e fu *O*   1472 d. si grant j. *OV*   1473 t. ci a. *O*
1475 Ke *not in OV*   1476 de m. en p. *O*   1477 serrez *O*   1478 enprise *OV*

1480 Ke vostre poeir la meintenge,
     Si la menez par le pais—
     Ben serra dreit, ceo me est avis—
     E ses puceles oveke li
1484 De bel atur, sachez de fi,
     Od palefreis beaus e grans e seins,
     Od beles robes, od beaus loreins,
     E vus averez les robes rustes,
1488 E en dette serrez deske as cutes.
     De ta femme vaut meuz la mustresun
     Ke tut l'estor de ta mesun.
     Si la femme vostre veisin
1492 Seit meuz vestue, sachez, sanz fin
     Vus criera sur e tost e tart
     E si dirra: "La male hart
     Vus pende, mauveis putre vilein,
1496 Quel ke ceo seit ui u demein,
     Car vus me hunissez entre gent
     Ke vus mei vestez si povrement.
     De ceo ke men est, trestut sanz faille,
1500 Vus ne i avez vaillant la maille.   259*d*
     Del men vus fetes si honorer,
     Ke jo en parte, ne poez endurer.
     N'ad nul si povre ici entur
1504 Ki a sa femme ne face mult grant honur,
     Fors vus ki estes un teu cheitif;
     Mar vint l'ure ke jo vus pris."
     Suvent vus recordera ceste lessun
1508 E si vus dorra sa maleisun.
     Quant la veistes al comencement,
     Quant vestue fu tresrichement,
     E les beaus aneaus par tut les deiz
1512 E ses ataches a beaus orfreiz

1508 dorrra si m.

1480 p. le m. *OV*   1483 sas p. *O*, ces p. *V*   1485 E p. b. g. e s. *O*; A p. b. g.
e s. *V*   1486 E b. r. e b. l. *O*   1487 la robes rutes *OV*   1488 E serrez en d. *O*;
a c. *OV*   1490 la stor, uostre m. *O*   1497 vus h. mei *OV*   1499 tut sanz f. *O*
1500 auez vileyn la m. *O*   1501 anurer *O*, anorer *V*   1502 part *O*; p. durer *V*
1504 a *not in O*; mult *not in OV*   1510 mut richement *V*

E le heritage ke li chei,
Mult quidiez poi, sachez de fi,
Ke tel semence e si amere
1516 Vus estuast en sa aumosnere.
Ore em pernez, si en maschez,
De tel en averez vus assez.
Iteu solaz e teu deport
1520 Ne vus faudra deskes a la mort.
Si issi est ke de ceste vie
Seit ta femme par tens partie,
Joier poez e plus suef vivere,
1524 Car de grant mal estes delivre.
Si de pleindre nen poez tenir,
Mult meillure vus poet avenir
Ke ele ne fu, sachez de veir.
1528 Lessez ester vostre doleir,
Si pensez ben ke vus estes humme,
Ne devez pas por chescune pumme
Plurer cum enfant mesaffeité.
1532 Ben le sachez de verité:
Ki ad femme de bone part,
Ceo est cheance cum de hasart.'   260a

LE VEILLARD

'Ben est veir,' fet li prudume;
1536 'La beneisun Deu e seint Pere de Rume
Pussez aver, mun tresduz fiz,
Por tun solaz e tes beaus diz,
Car en cest cas, ki fu mult dur,
1540 Mult me avez fet ben asseur.
Ore mei dites une demande avant,
Pus vus lerrai pes a itant,
Ceo est le tut: ke mun bon ami

1526 poez

1514 quidez *OV*   1517 si] e *OV*   1519 s. iteu confort *OV*   1525 ne p. *OV*
1526 poez *V*   1527 pur v. *OV*   1529 vus *not in OV*   1531 cum un e. *O*
1532 pur v. *V*; l'de *written above* pur *V*   1540 fet *not in O*   1541 me di *OV*
1542 pes autant *V*

1544 S'en est de cest secle parti,
      E jo en sui tut sul remis,
      Trop esgaree e entrepris.
      Si l'en me vousist mal espier,
1548 Jo ne savereie en ki fier.
      Sachez le vus, por icest cas
      Mun quor en est dolent e las.
      Nule perte, ceo savez ben,
1552 Vers perte de ami ne ateint a ren.'

                    L'ENFANT

      L'enfant respund: 'C'est un tresor
      Ki mult vaut meuz ke argent u or.
      La verité en avez vus dite:
1556 Perte de ami n'est pas petite.
      Resun ne i vei de trop doleir,
      Fors ke vus fetes vostre vuleir.
      Ke quidez vus par tun plurer
1560 Vostre bon ami resusciter?
      Ne poet estre, e dunc coment?
      Ne aviez fors celui sulement?'

                  LE VEILLARD

      'Nun!' fet li veil, 'de ceo me doil,
1564 Car jo l'amai cum mun destre oil.'

                    L'ENFANT

      'Par fai,' respundi idunc l'enfant,
      'Beaus sire cher, ceo est merveille grant
      Ke par un autre enz mi la mer
1568 Vuliez ta nef asseurer.
      Ceste mer ki est parfunde,

1561 poez   Le veillard *is beside l. 1563*, L'enfant *beside l. 1565*

1546 engarre O   1547 Si lum en mei v. *V*   1549 icel cas O   1554 mult *not in* O
1555 vus *not in* OV   1556 ne pas *V*   1557 i *not in* OV; veye O   1559 uostre
p. O   1563 men d. *V*   1565 respont *V*

Ki envirune tut le munde,
De la meité ne travaille mie
1572 Cum cest secle par felunie.
Dunc signefie cest mund la mer
Por le travail e l'encumbrer.
La mer ne fet ke fere ne deit,
1576 Mes icest mund nus tuz deceit.
Perilz de mer eschivrez suvent,
Les maus del mund ne sai coment.
Dunc di jeo ke les maus en terre
1580 Passent la mer en meint affere,
E vus, entre cent mile maus,
Seur vus fist un ami leaus.
Ceo est iceo ke jo vus dis avant:
1584 Par un autre futes waucrant.
Mult en poez aver grant hunte,
Si vostre valur nent plus ne amunte
Ke nen avez fors un ami
1588 De tant cum vus avez vesqui.
Si tut li autre sunt enemis,
Mester vus avereint cent mil e dis.
Ja tant n'averez, coment ke seit,
1592 Ke vers tanz maus mester n'i eit,
Ke si celui vus faut de sa,
Succurs vus frad icil de la;
Si serra vostre garnesture
1596 De tutes parz par aventure.'

LE VEILLARD

Li veil respund: 'Ceo est ben veir,
Mes jo vudrei mult bien saveir
Cument jo pusse a chef venir
1600 De ta promesse e de mun desir.
Car la aval des funz de abisme
Deske enz al cel vet la fausime.

1574 Par (p) *OV*   1575 La m. fet que f. deit *V*   1576 nus] vus *O*; tuz *not in O*
1577 eschium *V*   1580 e meint a. *O*   1588 nasquy *O*   1592 nel eyt *O*
1594 icest de la *OV*   1600 tun desir *OV*; p⁴messe *V*   1601 la val *V*; de f. *OV*
1602 Ieskes au c. *V*; est la f. *OV*

Por ceo ne sai de tuz eslire
1604 Ki meuz en vaut u seit le pire.
      Jo porrei mettre ma fiance
      U jo averei mauveis[e] cuvenance.   260c
      E la perte ai de mun cher ami;
1608 Ore ne pus saver en ki me fi.'

L'ENFANT

'Certes, sire, vus avez tort
Ke tant pleinnez iceste mort.
Ja nel pussez vus tant amer
1612 Ke vus ne truissez assez sun per,
      Si vus ussez le acointance
      Ke entre vus fust [e] l'aliance.
      Entre cinc cent mile des faus
1616 Poet l'em trover aukun leaus.
      Por ceo vus facez de tuz amer,
      Aucun vus en porra aver mester.
      Tu as perdu tun bon ami,
1620 Aviez unkes mester de li?'

LE VEILLARD

'Nenal,' fet cil, 'mes de sun semblant
E de sa promesse me alai vantant.
Issi l'avei jo ben espruvé,
1624 Unc plus leal ne fu trové.'

L'ENFANT

L'enfant respunt: 'Sire prudum,
Si sages fussez cum Salomon,
Vus en porriez estre deceu
1628 De un bon ami ben conu.

L'enfant *is beside l. 1609*

1604 la p. *OV*   1606 mauueyse c. *OV*   1608 ma fi *V*   1610 icest m. *O*
1613 la a. *O*   1614 fust la a. *O*   1615 c. c. e mil de f. *V*   1621 fet il *V*
1622 p᷑messe men alai *V*   1623 jo *not in V*   1626 cum fu S. *O*

Tuz ne sunt pas amis verrais
Ki vus losengent de dous en treis.
Ki beit e mangue a ta table
1632 Ne serra ami covenable,
Si assaé ne l'as avant;
Mar le crerras ne tant ne quant.
Car ceus ki plus vus promettereint,
1636 A chef de tur vus decever[e]int;
Teus juent e bel vus rient,
Al paraler de vus mesdient.
Cil vus aiment e pres e loin,
1640 Mes il vus faudrunt al grant busoin.
Ceo est le amisté de mein en mein:
Tant as, tant vaus, e tant vus aim.   *260d*
De teus en averez vus assez,
1644 Deske les eez ben espruvez;
Amis vus serrunt deskes en terre
Tant cum vus lur porrer nul ben fere.
Si mester avez de lur aie,
1648 Perdue averez lur cumpaignie.
A l'envesprer lue l'en [le] jur,
Si fet l'em de ami la grant amur.
Mes tun ami ke tant amastes,
1652 Unkes en busoin ne l'espruvastes,
Poet cel estre k'il vus faudreit,
Quant il vus plus aider devreit.
Dunc di jo ben ke vus avez tort,
1656 Quant ne vulez aver cunfort
De tun ami ki en busoin
Ne vus fist regard ne pres ne loin.
Querez vostre ami, si li espruvez,
1660 E quant vus ben leal le truvez,
Meintenez le, si fras ke sage;
Tut li dirrez vostre curage
E il a vus, e vus a li,

1630 de d. u t. O   1632 ami pas c. O   1635 plus *not in* OV; prometterunt V
1636 deceuerunt V   1637 Teus venint V   1638 A p. V   1640 Mes cil, a
g. b. V   1644 D. vus les eez O   1646 Tant ke vus O   1649 envespreye O; l.
len le j. OV   1652 en un b. V   1654 Qua O   1657 boloyn O   1658 f. r.
pres V   1660 vus *not in* V   1661 frez OV   1662 durrez O   1663 Cil a uus V

1664 Dunc serrez vus le soen ami.
E si plus de un poez gainner,
Plus en poez asseurer
Cuntre les maus de ceste vie,
1668 Ke tant est pleine de tricherie.
De ure en autre, de jur en jur,
Mult en dussez aver pour,
Ne mie doleir, savez por quei?
1672 Jo le vus dirrai en bone fei:
Tant cum vus en joirez plus,
Tant serrunt vos enemis cunfus.
Si vus en dulez de nule ren,
1676 Il en rierunt, sachez le ben.
Si ma priere poet ren valeir,
Jo vus toudrai icest duleir.   261a
Regardez ben vostre nessance
1680 E la vie de vostre enfance:
Le meillur ami, quant futes né,
Si fu cele ke vus out porté
Dis meis en sun ventre demeine
1684 E mult por vus suffri grant peine;
Unkes pus tel nen aviez
Pus cel ure ke futes nez.
Issi pleint l'em les adventiz
1688 Plus ke ne fet sa mere le fiz.
Par duçur e par debonerté
Fu primes tun ami porchacé,
De vus vint primes la encheisun
1692 Ke il vus ama tant par reisun;
Ta grant valur e ta franchise
De vus amer li fist l'emprise.
Par mauvesté e par felunie
1696 Sanz ami serriez tute ta vie.
Sachez ke leal ami atret
Vostre grant ben ki bon le fet,

1665 E si de un plus p. *OV*   1666 enseurer *OV*   1667 le m. *V*   1672 le *not in O*
1673 en *not in O*, ioyerez *O*   1676 riereyent *O*, rierent *V*   1687 enuentis *OV*
1688 ne fet fauz mere *O*   1691 len encheisun *V*   1692 il *not in O*   1693 Ta v.
e ta grant fr. *O*; Tant g. v. e tant grant fr. *V*   1696 serrez *OV*

Dunc estes vus li menestrel

1700 Ki fet le ami de home mortel.

Si vostre ami seit ore mort,

Vus devez aver mult grant cunfort

Ke li mestre uncore vit

1704 Ke si bon ami avant le fist.

Ne devez pas dunc desesperer,

Quant nen as ubblié vostre mester

De fere un ami, jofne u chanu,

1708 Autresi bon cum celui fu.

Ceo semble ben ke seit enfance

De doleir por tele meses[tan]ce;   261b

Vus ne i gainnerez a chef de tur

1712 Fors pesantume de ta dolur.'

LE VEILLARD

'Ben poet estre,' fet il, 'beau frere;

Iceste vie, ke tant est amere

Sulunc vos diz, nent plus ne amunte

1716 Fors por vostre vie mettre a hunte.

De Deu seez vus beneit, beau fiz.

Meuz le vei ore ke einz ne fiz

Par ta reisun e par tun dit.

1720 Preiser en poum nus mult petit

Les aventures de ceste vie,

Car mei semblereit mult grant folie

Suffrir une mesaventure

1724 E doleir trop a desmesure.

En l'un avereit assez de mal

De fere un anguisse cural.

Ore ne [vus] sai jo nent plus dire,

1728 Car vus m[e s]avez ben descunfire.

Par mun seig[nur s]eint Pere le apostre,

Ore seit la mestrie tut vostre.

1700 homo   *The square brackets in ll. 1710, 1727–9, 1761 indicate effacement of letters in L*

1705 pas *not in* O*V*; de esperer *V*   1709 ben *not in* O*V*   1710 d. de tel m. O*V*
1715 nen plus *V*   1716 por *not in V*   1720 Penser O*V*; mult *not in V*
1722 semblerent O; mult *not in* O*V*   1724 e a desmesure O   1727 vus *not in* O*V*
1730 trestute la m. vostre O

Encuntre sen e cuntre reisun
1732 Ne dei par dreit aver fuisun.
Nel vus di pas par cuverture,
Mult ad en vus sen e mesure.
Ki me deist ke jofne leger
1736 Ne deit sen ne resun aver,
Jo li desmentireie sanz faille,
Car sanz dute ceste bataille
Me ad fet trover ceo ke jo quis:
1740 En jofne age sen ben assis.
Des ore voil cunseiller les veuz,
Si il se voelent tenir al meuz,   261c
Ke il ne blament a desmesure
1744 Jofne por sa bele enveisure.
Beau duz fiz, a vus me rent,
Vus me dirrez vostre talent,
Ceo ke vus vulez ke jo face
1748 Fors ke jo aie la vostre grace.'

L'ENFANT

L'enfant respund: 'Vostre merci
Del ben ke me avez dit ici.
Si sen i ad e Deus i mist,
1752 Ki le cors e l'alme fist,
Deu le meintenge, si lu plest,
E cresse en ben, en joie e en het.
Sire prudum, e vus si face,
1756 Deu vus doint la sue grace.
Cunfortez vus ben, si seez lee,
Tan[t] cum vus avera Deu destinee,
Si cum fet iceste flur
1760 Ki ben veez ici entur.
Ceo semble ke ce[ste pr]aerie,
Ke pert ore si ben flurie,

1731 e *not in* V; encuntre r. OV   1734 Mut est en vus O   1737 dementirai V
1739 tr. ore cest, ore *expuncted* V   1742 Si il le veylle t. O; Si se voillent t. a m. V
1744 la bele e. O   1747 vus *not in* OV; voillez V   1748 jo, la *not in* OV   1750 me
not in O   1754 e en j. O   1755 Si p. V   1756 doine V   1757 vus *not in* V;
e seez le O

U ke ele eit joie mult parfite,
1764 U en sa manere se delite.
Por ceo n'ad le hume gueres de tort,
Si il se peine de aver cunfort.
E vus ne vus esmaez de ren,
1768 Par mun cunseil, fetes le ben.
Requerez le fiz seinte Marie
Ke il garisse la vostre vie
En joie e en ben, sanz encumbrer,
1772 Ki poet e set tut guverner,
E vus doint poeir de lu servir,
E en sun servise ben meintenir,   261*d*
E vus doint aver bone fin
1776 E a lui aler le dreit chemin,
E vus e nus e tut li vif
Ki averunt oi icest estrif.
Amen, amen, chescun en die.
1780 Ore nus ait seinte Marie.' Amen.

1763 mult *not in OV*   1765 de *not in O*   1766 il *not in V*   1770 Ke nus e uus
tut iours guie *V*   1770–1 *telescoped* Ke sanz encumbrer pussez viure *O*   1774 E
eynz sun s. *O*   1775 doinst *V*   1776 a *not in O*   1777 E nus e vus *OV*; le vif *V*
1779 en *not in V*   1780 Ore nus ait tuz le fiz M. *O*   Explicit liber qui vocatur
peti ple *V*

NOTES

4. entredalierent For a commentary on the etymology and semantic development of this word in Anglo-Norman, see L. Spitzer, *Romania* 75 (1954), 390–5. Here the sense is 'debate, discuss'.

5. juvente I hesitate between *t* and *c* in this reading.

10. tus 'young man'. Koch postulates *iuventosus to explain *jofnetus* which he writes as one word. *LO* both show a division into two words while *V* gives *iuventus*. The etymon is surely *tonsum*, though the R.E.W. and F.E.W. quote only Provençal examples of a masculine form. T.-L. 4, 1705, accepts *jofnetus* on the basis of this one example.

14. ventage A derivative of *ventus*, presumably meaning 'trifle'. The F.E.W. 14, 261 gives *ventaige* mfr. 'vent, tempête'.

16. Koch interprets **ben assis** as 'well presented' which he makes an attributive of **diz**. This means he must explain **de** twice as a partitive. It is more likely that **assis** means 'provided with' (cf. T.-L. 1, 586.6) and that **ben** is a noun not an adverb.

25. del mund 'in this world'.

33. de l'autrui would normally mean 'from the property of others', hence the reading of *V* seems more regular.

37–8. The forms **leres, tricheres** suggest that the four nouns in these lines are singular. The change of determinant from **les** with plural nouns in 35–6 to **li** in 37–8 seems also to indicate intentional distinction between the two groups.

38. faus pleidur, tricheres Both were legal terms, see Edouard Meynial, *Mélanges Chabaneau* (Erlangen, 1907), 559, 562.

43. dunt si tuché vus ai 'to whom I referred'; cf. *Boeve de Haumtone*, ed. A. Stimming (Halle, 1899), l. 847; Gdf. 10, 783b.

47–53. Assuming that **rendreit plet** *LO* 50 is a synonym for *tendreit plet* *V*, it seems possible to make sense of this passage only by interverting 49 and 50, in spite of the agreement of *LOV* (cf. the interversion of 1379–80 in *OV*), and by understanding **ne** 51 as **nel**. The passage would then mean: 'that sorrow would never dwell in his heart, and that he would never take any account of this fleeting world; if God did not so far care to look after him that he changed his ideas, he was determined to think only of himself'. Koch has *tendreit* 50 and rejects *ne* 51 (*LOV*) in favour of *le* on the basis of *Set Dormanz* 14: *si . . . (E) Deu nus vousist itant tenser*. He translates 47–52 (p. 203): 'Er sagte, dass der schmerz dieser unbeständigen welt in seinem herzen keine stätte haben würde und er ihn für nichts achten wollte, wenn gott ihm (dem jüngling) insofern helfen wollte, dass er sein sinnen und denken bessere.'

52. Koch reads *amendust V*.

66–8. Cf. Introduction, p. xxvi.

69. de meinte manere 'in great variety'.

90. Koch reads *pdom L.*

93. To keep *icel L,* it would have to be assumed that **dolur** was masculine (cf. *Horn* II, note on l. 3545).

96. **despleise**   See Introduction, p. xxvi.

103. **bainet**   See Introduction p. xxiii and Pope §1295(i).

110. The construction **por** + gerund is not common; see E. Gamillscheg, *Historische Französische Syntax* (Tübingen, 1957), p. 445.

113–18. Cf. *Disticha Catonis* I, 16:

> Multorum cum facta senex et dicta reprendis,
> fac tibi succurrant iuvenis quae feceris ipse.

Cf. also *Josaphaz* 577–83 (quoted Introduction, p. xxx).

116. **bel age**   A euphemism for middle age? Cf. 441.

143. **ke** 'who'.

150. T.-L. 5, 233 under **latin** gives 'Kunst, Wissenschaft' and Gdf. 4, 736a 'finesse, ruse, subtilité'. The line presumably means: 'And it would be an unintelligent, unwise thing....'

155–6. *Disticha Catonis* III, 6:

> Interpone tuis interdum gaudia curis,
> ut possis animo quemvis sufferre laborem.

173–4. Cf. Morawski 201: 'Aussi tost meurt veiaux com vaiche.'

177. **e munt [e] jus**   This rare combination is not noted by L. Foulet in 'L'Effacement des adverbes de lieu', *Romania* 69 (1946–7), 1–79, and T.-L. lists only one other example, 'que d'amont que de jus', *La Mort Aymeri de Narbonne,* S.A.T.F. (1884), l. 630.

183. 'you could teach him a thing or two about it'.

192. **de plus** appears to have the same meaning as *plus*; see A. Tobler, *Vermischte Beiträge* 2 (2nd ed., Leipzig, 1906), 62–4.

193. Koch reads *moire V,* an error caused by a crease in the page.

200. **Ki** 'those whom'.

201. **les** refers to *les veuz.*

204. The position of **i** is unusual.

205–7. 'Because of their ills and troubles, they (old people) have to be looked after by someone else, just as a nurse does a child, ...'

208. **danzelant** 'pampering'. Not a derivative of *tanzen* as Koch supposed, but from **domnicella* (T.-L. 2, 1187).

217–18. There are two comparisons involved in this construction, both dependent on **Meus me vaut mort.** For the use of the subjunctive in the second, see Gamillscheg, op. cit., pp. 748–9.

220. 'which would be with me for an unhappy period of time'.

230. **demeine**   See Introduction, pp. xxvi–xxvii.

249. **beaut** < *bald* not < *bellum*; cf. 930 and note.

251. *porriet L* has been corrected to **porreit** to avoid possible confusion with *t* for *z* in the second person plural; see Introduction, p. xxiii.

272. Koch suggests (p. 207) that **vostre** could be changed to *nostre,* if **vie** is interpreted as human life in general.

277. *li* is used for **le** by the scribe of *L*. As this is not a known Anglo-Norman trait, I have preferred the *V* reading *le*.

281. **freez** Cf. *resteez*, *Set Dormanz* 1108; see Tanquerey, op. cit., pp. 212–13 and Morphology, p. xxiii.

294. Koch reads *muscer* L.

298. Koch reads *fu* for *su* O (*sui V*).

301. A proverbial expression; see T.-L. 2, 385.

314. The rejection of *mort* L for **morir** (*OV murir*) avoids assuming that **estoet** is here used personally, an unlikely possibility (cf. T.-L. 3, 1431).

342. **vuler** Cf. Introduction, p. xxiii.

345. Neither the figurative use of **gué** here, nor the use in 587, is noted by Gdf. or T.-L.

349–51. Cf. Seneca, *De remediis fortuitorum* (Palmer, op. cit., p. 32):

> *Ratio*. Nec primus: vltimus omnes me antecesserunt, omnesque consequentur.

362. Cf. Seneca (Palmer, op. cit., p. 30):

> *Ratio*. Peregrenatio est vita, multa cum deambulaueris: deinde redeundum est.

366. Koch reads *dunc* for *dune* O.

367–72. 'There is not a man on earth, he said, who as a reproach could tell you that you will die sooner or later, who would not have his share in death. Since the son of God suffered death, it is wrong for you to fear it.'

378. **greinnur** 'greatest'.

379–81. Seneca (Palmer, op. cit., p. 34):

> *Sensus*. Sed saepe ferieris et multi in te gladii concurrent.

389. Cf. Seneca (Palmer, op. cit., p. 34):

> *Ratio*. Quid refert an multa sint vulnera non potest amplius, quam vnum esse mortiferum.

391. The *OV* variant *home* seems to be a better reading, but **Jesu** makes acceptable sense; cf. 371.

397. **Lessez . . . a cunvenir** 'let . . . take care of matters'. Here and in 856 the MS. readings appear to be **a cunvenir** rather than **acunvenir** which Koch prints. Since *acunvenir*, though not entirely unattested as Koch says (cf. T.-L. 1, 122.40), appears to be very rare, and since *lesser cunvenir* is frequently found (T.-L. 2, 984), I have preferred the simple verb. This means accepting the construction *lesser* + *a* + inf. (T.-L. 5, 89.32).

404. 'a single foot of land'.

415. Cf. Seneca (Palmer, op. cit., p. 34):

> *Sensus*. Peregre morieris.

421. **moerc** *L* reads *moert* which I have changed, as it is more reasonable to assume a velar ending; cf. Pope § 900.

429. **trop** 'in great numbers'.

440. The reading of *L* seems to be **itute** not **i tute** which Koch reads (cf. *V itote*). However this does not render the line much less obscure and I can offer no suitable translation. Koch conjectures that the original might have been *en tute volunté*.

445. Cf. *Vulgate*, Gen. 3:19: 'quia pulvis es, et in pulverem reverteris'.

451. **le quel est tel** 'which is which'. I have not noted this expression elsewhere.

453. **Inde** Cf. *Josaphaz* 1982: 'En Inde n'en nule autre terre'.

461–2. Cf. Seneca (Palmer, op. cit., p. 34):

Ratio. Non est grauior foris: quam domi somnus.

479. An earlier scribe probably copied **se tint** from 480 instead of writing *se tut*. This error is common to all MSS.; see Introduction, p. xvii.

482, 484. If the *L* reading is kept, **i** can be taken to mean 'in the matter' 482, 'in what he says' 484. It is possible to emend to *le V*; cf. 277.

496–8. 'whatever country you are in will be yours, even if you are not worth a halfpenny'. For the general sense, cf. 517–18, 523–7.

511–13. 'Not even in your father's house will you have perfect joy nor any help from kinsman or mother. . . .'.

530. Cf. 'S'il fet folie, si la boive'; 'Ensi com il brassa si but'; 'Con avés brasé, si bevés', T.-L. 1, 1040 and 1107.

532. It is possible that the comma should be after **Sachez** or **le**, 'remains a good thing in itself'.

539–40. 'Therefore it is everywhere pleasant to be, if one makes wisdom one's master'.

554. Cf. Seneca (Palmer, op. cit., p. 36):

Sensus. Iuuenis morieris.

558. 'and a great misfortune that would take away my joy'.

562–6. 'for it would be no joke for you to be born thus and to die young (so) that you could not enjoy this ephemeral life more than an old man (would)'.

581. **mult** The author may have written *meuz* (cf. 589), although all MSS. have **mult**; cf. 607 where *meuz* would be much more logical than *bon*. See discussion of manuscript filiation, p. xvii. However, there is a similar construction, apparently lacking a comparative adverb, in the Latin of the Vulgate: 'expedit enim tibi ut pereat unum membrorum tuorum, quam totum corpus tuum mittatur in gehennam', Matt. 5:29 (and similarly in 5:30). Chardri may be adopting this construction from a familiar Biblical passage, with *ke* equivalent to *quam* in the sense of 'rather than'.

587. Cf. note on 345.

603–6. I have found no exact parallel to this passage.

605. Koch prints *Se* for **Ke**, which Mussafia, op. cit., p. 606, declares

unnecessary. Mussafia does not see the subjunctive as unusual; cf. Introduction, p. xxvi.

607. Cf. note on 581.

610. Cf. note on 530.

616. **espeir** 'expectation'. The line appears to mean 'give me something to look forward to, to cheer me up'.

622. Cf. Seneca (Palmer, op. cit., p. 36):

Sensus. Insepultus eris.

629 ff. Cf. Seneca (Palmer, op. cit., p. 38):

Ratio. . . , an fera me commedat, . . .

648. **bleste** 'clod'. For a discussion of the etymology, see F. Lecoy, *Romania* 75 (1954), 413.

655. One would expect *Ke nul voille*; cf. Introduction, p. xxvii.

661-8. Cf. Seneca (Palmer, op. cit., p. 40):

Ratio. . . , non defunctorum causa: sed viuorum inuenta est sepultura, vt corpora et visu, et odore feda amouerentur, . . .

672-3. 'and people would live much less long than they once did'.

678. Tanquerey, op. cit., p. 500, reconstructs this line from *OV* as *Mes* (or *Mut*) *de poi estes esmeu*. Both seem unlikely and it is possible that Tanquerey was more concerned with the question of re-establishing diaeresis for *esmeu* than considering the sense.

682. Cf. Job 12:12:

In antiquis est sapientia, et in multo tempore prudentia.

689-90. 'no matter how much he has heard and seen, he can yet be considered a fool'. See also Introduction, p. xxvi.

696. Koch suggests (p. 212) that this line has a meaning similar to 697, however I feel that **assez** and **plus** refer back to **aventures** 693: 'the dead have plenty (of misfortunes) and the living more'.

711. **voil comencer** A future construction according to E. Burghardt, *Über den Einfluss des Englischen auf das Anglonormannische*, Studien zur Englischen Philologie 24 (Halle, 1906), pp. 69, 72; cf. 459, 1742.

712. This line which appears in both *L* and *O* has no obvious sense. Perhaps the line was originally a game-playing formula meaning 'It doesn't matter who has the first go', here taken as 'It doesn't matter which point I begin with', admittedly a speculative interpretation. Koch adopts the *V* reading *E puis i verrez quei amounte* which may well have been invented by a scribe who was himself confronted with a difficult line.

713. **lie** 'integral, unavoidable fault, drawback', (contrasting with **sein**). This figurative use is somewhat like the expression 'De melancolie dient il ke c'est li lie dou sanc', Amédée Salmon, 'Remèdes populaires du moyen âge' in *Etudes romanes dédiées à Gaston Paris* (Paris, 1891), p. 254(1).

732-6. Cf. Seneca (Palmer, op. cit., p. 40):

Ratio. Venit tempus, quo experimentum mei caperem non in mari tantum, aut in prelio vir fortis apparet, exhibitur etiam lectulo virtus.

Koch considered 733 an example of the author's interest in chivalry, but the close parallel with Seneca seems to contradict this.

735. 'I will not refrain from telling you'; or 'I cannot help but tell you'.

742–6. Cf. Seneca (Palmer, op. cit., pp. 40–2):

> *Ratio.* Non potest illud toto saeculo fieri, aut ego febrem relinquam: aut ipsa me, semper vna esse non possumus. Cum morbo mihi res est, aut vincitur, aut vincet.

752. 'in illness or perhaps in battle'.

757. The reading of *L Cum ja haschee* is simply a slip of the pen.

775. Cf. Seneca (Palmer, op. cit., p. 42):

> *Sensus.* Male de te opinantur homines.

778. In *OV* **ke** is a relative, 'that I shall not have deserved', but in *L* a conjunction, 'in such circumstances that I shall not have deserved it', i.e. 'without my deserving it'.

784. **il**= **le produme** 782; **li** = **un fol** 781.

786–92. Cf. *Disticha Catonis* III, 2:

> Cum recte vivas, ne cures verba malorum:
> arbitrii non est nostri quid quisque loquatur.

787. **en dous e en treis** 'indiscriminately, equally' (?), cf. *de dous en treis* 1630 and T.-L. 2, 1845.47.

797–800. Cf. Seneca (Palmer, op. cit., p. 42):

> *Ratio.* Sed mali, mouerer si de me Marius, si Cato, si Laelius sapiens, si aliter Cato, si duo Scipiones ista loquerentur, . . .

798. **devriez** 'would have reason to'. In *V* Koch reads *Vus deu⁴ez* as *Tus deivez*.

799. Cf. *Josaphaz* 7, 'Augustin u de seint Gregoire'.

809. See Introduction, p. xxvii.

815–16. Proverbial?

821. The *kar* of *OV* seems to imply that the **ke** of *L* is co-ordinating 'for', not subordinating 'that' depending on **sachez**.

829–30. 'they will not be able to do great harm, even though they say foolish things'.

837–8. Proverbial; cf. Morawski 1514 'Len ne puet faire de buisart espervier', also 96, 965 and T.-L. 1, 1197–8.

843. **vulez crere** Burghardt, op. cit., pp. 51, 57, 63, sees this and the examples in 1037, 1414 (and possibly 1459, 1742) as circumlocutions of the simple verb. However, it is doubtful whether any of the cases he mentions should be so taken.

849. **Ennuuse** Koch prints *enviuse* from *OV*. The *Perceval* 1241 has *enuiouse* with *lange*.

854. Some hesitation in the transcription of **estuper** is caused by a dot at the top of the stem of *p*, making the word at first appear as *estirper*, a variant of *estreper*.

856. Cf. 397 and note.

864. **ses** = *ces*.

865. I have interpreted **sanz fin** here and in 1492 in the accepted sense of 'continually'. However, one wonders, given its appearance each time with **sachez** and the fact that in 1492 enjambement is necessary to keep the usual sense, whether *sanz fin* could mean 'indeed, in truth'.

878. The construction is somewhat elliptical, as the sense of 'command' which is negatively expressed by **defendu** 876 must be understood positively here, that is with the sense of 'recommend'.

881. The reading of *L* is at first sight *annile* (so Koch), but a close examination shows a stain on the manuscript which gives the impression of lengthening the second minim of the *u*.

890. *Disticha Catonis* I, 21:

> Infantem nudum cum te natura crearit,
> paupertatis onus patienter ferre memento.

Cf. also J. Morawski, *Les Diz et Proverbes des Sages* (Paris, 1924), p. 64, CXCI:

> Tout nud fuz nez de ta propre nature,
> Riens n'apportas: tout gist en aventure.

903. I have found no exact parallel for this proverb.

906. 'Take not too much thought for the morrow on this account'.

910. The meaning appears to be 'So God is giving me a gift that has dangers attached'. The proverb 'Dieus done le buef, més ce n'est pas par la corne' (Morawski 580) is rendered by Cotgrave (s.v. *boeuf*) 'God gives things plentifully and without perill'.

921. **en wrec** 'in penury, uncared for'.
One would expect *nel larrad*, though all MSS. have **ne larrad**. See Introduction, p. xvii.

923–6. Cf. Seneca (Palmer, op. cit., p. 48):

> *Ratio.* Nihil deest auibus, pecora in diem viuunt. Feris ad alimenta sollicitudo sua sufficit.

926. 'they do not know on what they will dine'. The *V* reading is *dismer* according to Koch. The scribe has certainly written *f*, perhaps in error.

930. **beauz** 'gay' < *bald*; cf. 249 and note.

939–40. Cf. *Vulgate*, Ecclesiasticus 3: 22:

> Altiora te ne quaesieris, et fortiora te ne scrutatus fueris; sed, quae praecepit tibi Deus, illa cogita semper et in pluribus operibus ejus ne fueris curiosus;
>
> 23. non est enim tibi necessarium ea quae abscondita sunt videre oculis tuis.
>
> 24. In supervacuis rebus noli scrutari multipliciter, et in pluribus operibus ejus non eris curiosus.

940. **le meins** 'all the less'. 943. **le plus** 'all the more'. This is a

possible Anglicism; cf. A. Tobler, *Vermischte Beiträge* 2 (2nd ed., Leipzig, 1906), 57–9; cf. also A. Stimming, *Der anglonormannische Boeve de Haumtone* (Halle, 1899), note on l. 2701.

951–5. 'And if you cannot refrain from complaining—for that can easily happen—it does not matter, provided that your plaint does not at any cost reveal your very inmost thoughts'.

961–4, 971–2. Cf. Seneca (Palmer, op. cit., p. 48):

> *Ratio.* Vtrum auarus, aut prodigus: si auarus nil habet, sin prodigus, nil habebit: . . .

For this whole passage, cf. also *Disticha Catonis* IV, 16:

> Utere quaesitis opibus, fuge nomen avari:
> quid tibi divitiae, si semper pauper abundes?

and in similar vein, IV, 1:

> Despice divitias, si vis animo esse beatus;
> quas qui suspiciunt, mendicant semper avari.

962, 971. **fous large, foularge** 'spendthrift, prodigal'. In each case, these are printed as they stand in the base MS.

967. The construction is elliptical. For the sense in English, one must understand a phrase such as 'will insist on'.

972. 'it will not last him long'. The fut.3 of both *durer* and *duner* in MS. L is **dorra**.

979. **wandelarz** 'swindlers'? Three other examples of this word are known. In 'A Song of the Times', Thomas Wright, *The Political Songs of England* (London, 1839), p. 49, it appears in Latin: 'Hic sunt fratres quatuor Robertus et Ricardus, Gilebertus postea, vir valde *Wandelardus* . . .' The meaning from the context is unclear, but 'deceiver, cheat' (since *Gilebert* is later punningly associated with *gilur*) is suggested by Koch (pp. 214–15). Lucy Toulmin Smith and Paul Meyer note it in *Les Contes moralisés de Nicole Bozon*, S.A.T.F. 8 (1889), conte 63, p. 86: 'Plusours gentz sont semblables a *wandelardz* qe sont par lur trespaz cheüz en la merci lur seignour . . .', but their explanation (p. 256) adds nothing to Bozon's text. The word also occurs in English in Peter Langtoft's *Chronicle*, ed. Thomas Hearne (Oxford, 1725) I, 115: 'þise men lift þer standard þat stout was & grim, Ageyn David *wandelard*, & disconfite him', for which Stratmann in his *Middle English Dictionary* gives '?vagabond, ?criminal'. Wright connects the word with *Vandal* and Koch tentatively suggests O.H.G. *wantal* (p. 215). From the *Petit Plet* context alone, one might co-ordinate the sense with **bailifs** and **viscuntes**, hence 'official' of some kind, but the other occurrences suggest some sort of swindler or criminal.

986. **cuntee** is probably a variant of *contec* 'dispute' which is sometimes found in association with *plet* (cf. T.-L. 2, 758). The original rhyme could therefore have been *travillés* (m. sg. nom.) : *conté(c)s* (obl. pl.).

987. Cf. *Disticha Catonis* IV, 5:

> Cum fueris locuples, corpus curare memento:
> aeger dives habet nummos, se non habet ipsum.

994. Koch rejects **perdre**, the reading in all MSS., in favour of *perdra*. However, this is perhaps another example of the author's predilection for the infinitive; cf. Introduction, p. xxvii.

999. **Si** 'Supposing'. The **E** of 1003 would then best be translated as 'then'.

1007 ff. Cf. *Disticha Catonis* IV, 35:

> Ereptis opibus noli maerere dolendo,
> sed gaude potius, tibi si contingat habere.

1013. Koch prints the line as it stands in *V* (with regularized spelling) but notes (p. 215) that it should read *Ke huni ne vus ad ne ledenge*. Both **hunie** and **ledengee** appear to be feminine as the latter rhymes with **changee,** a probable instance of past participles agreeing with their subject; cf. *Horn* II, 91; cf. also Introduction, p. xxv.

1023–7. See Introduction, p. xxvii.

1026. Cf. *Disticha Catonis* III, 9:

> Cum tibi divitiae superant in fine senectae,
> munificus facito vivas, non parcus, amicis.

1027. **murdrir** 'conceal' (T.-L. 6, 262); cf. *murdri, Set Dormanz* 774.

1029. **Cist** 'such a man'.

1043. **u devendra** 'what will become of . . . ?'

1048. **E il** *OV* give *Cil* and Mussafia, op. cit., p. 606, reads *Cil* for *L*. None the less I read with Koch *E il*.

1060–2. Cf. Seneca (Palmer, op. cit., p. 52):

> *Ratio.* Nempe quam vt tu haberes, alius perdiderat.

1065. **volage** is here a noun, 'levity'; cf. *Set Dormanz* 297, 431 and Koch's note to *S.D.* 297.

1071–2. 'relieved me of my anxiety in this matter'.

1080–1. Cf. Seneca (Palmer, op. cit., p. 54):

> *Sensus.* Amisi liberos.

1085–6. **munde: amunte** Only the *V* reading *mund : amount* has what was probably the original rhyme. *Mund* and *munt* are known from early Old French, while *amount* suggests the suppression of final atonic *e*; cf. Pope §§ 1135, 1293.

1113–14. 'It is foolish and repugnant for a mortal man to bemoan the death of another'. Cf. Seneca (Palmer, op. cit., p. 54):

> *Ratio.* Stultus es si defles mortem mortalium.

1117. **est** Koch prefers *OV estes* which suits metre and sense better than *L*.

1119–24. Cf. Seneca (Palmer, op. cit., p. 54):

> *Ratio*. . . . Et hic tuus fructus est, ducuntur ex plebaea domo funera, ducuntur et ex regia.

1133. **dune** 'gives (him) the desire'. I have found no parallel to this use.

1140. **fors parti** 'excluded'. Koch translates 1139–40: 'When the king dies, he departs like the weakest, the least important person' and notes 'he has lived in vain, if he has left no heir'. However, in the context the passage more probably means: 'When he (the king) dies, the weakest will be excluded', because a struggle will inevitably ensue if there is no heir.

1157. **demeintenant** usually means 'immediately' (Gdf. 2, 493a). Perhaps **demeintenant quant** = 'as soon as, when'; thus 1157–8: 'did it depend on you to engender a child when you wished?'

1165–7. Cf. Seneca (Palmer, op. cit., p. 56):

> *Ratio*. . . . Educandos tibi fortuna mandauit, recepit illos, non abstulit.

1182. Cf. Seneca (Palmer, op. cit., p. 60):

> *Sensus*. Vxorem bonam amisi.

1184. **De ceo doler en ai grant dreit** The **de** in this line serves a dual function, *ai dreit de doler de ceo*, 'I have good reason to grieve because of this'.

1199–1200. 'I shall sooner die than be such a miserable wretch after she is gone'.

1201. **Mes** The variant *Mun OV* suggests that this might be a possessive adjective, but if so it would be the only example in the text of this form for the masc. sg. nom.

1214. 'it is no wonder if fools trust them (i.e. women)'. The reference seems to shift about in this passage from the old man's wife (1213, 1215–16) to women in general (1214, 1217 ff.).

1215–16. 'Even if she was (to begin with) wise, beautiful and courteous, she would be (exceptionally) good if she did not become evil (later on)'. Perhaps **deveneist** could be ind. impf.

1233. **wanelaces** 'devious, cunning tricks'. *O wenelaces, V wenlaces*. It is, remarks the O.E.D. under *wanlace*, 'not unlikely that it may be a Norman pronunciation of some native English word'. However, no satisfactory etymology has yet been found. The O.E.D. gives for *wanlace* (and the later alteration *windlass* sb. 2) the primary meaning of a circuit made to intercept the game in hunting, hence the figurative meaning of a circuitous course of action, a crafty device.

1237–8. '(You can) believe her and be certain (only) when she is openly malicious towards you'.

1241. Obviously proverbial, though I have found no parallel in English or French. It is perhaps similar to the basis of the phrase *entre chien et loup* which Cotgrave explains as 'when a man can hardly discerne a dog from a wolfe' (cf. F.E.W. 2, 197a). It would be just as wrong to consider all women to be the same as to see no difference between the two animals mentioned.

1245. en cresse Possibly one word, but a comparison with 1754 favours two.

1255. mar + subjunctive = negative imperative, E. Lerch, *Historische Französische Syntax* 3 (Leipzig, 1934), 107.

1271–2. See p. xxxi, n. 5.

1275. de mult 'for many things'.

1280–1. I have not found an exact parallel in English or French.

1282. The *L* reading is *Keke li eit* which I have emended to **Kek'il i eit** on the basis of *queke il i eit* 1427. One could print *Kek'el i eit* if it were assumed that *el* was for *ele*, not found elsewhere in this text, referring to *amur* fem.

1296–8. 'death has cut short her career so that she should not henceforth change her heart like February of the thirteen moods'.

1298. Cum feverer tredze covenant *O tresƷe, V treƷe*. Koch interprets *O tresƷe* as a variant of *trece, treche < trecier, trechier*, variants of *trichier*, but admits that he cannot account for the spellings of *L* and *V*. Miss L. W. Stone has pointed out to me that **tredze** is in fact the numeral 'thirteen', here used to indicate a large but indeterminate number (cf. *quatorƷe* in *Yvain* 441), while **covenant** means 'character, attitude', hence 'like February of the thirteen moods, ever-changing February'. For the general sense of the locution and its application to women, cf. 'Fame est le jor de tel semblanz, Fame a non .xiii. couvenanz', *Le Blame des Fames* in A. Jubinal, *Jongleurs et Trouvères* (Paris, 1835), p. 81; for the changeable character of February, cf. 'Hom plus crere ne la (Fortune) puet Ke feverer ki vente e pluet', in Simund de Freine's *Rom. de Phil.* (ed. Matzke), ll. 123–4, and *The Oxford Dictionary of English Proverbs*, s.v. *February*.

The form *covenant* is presumably the result of case or number confusion.

1299. engleter < **aquilentum* + *-ier*. The O.F. form was normally *aiglentier*, the A.N. form *eglenter* (as in *O*); by assimilation we get *englenter* (as in *V*) and *engleter* by dissimilation of this latter form. A woman is compared to a wild rose flower probably because of the thorns (unseen bad qualities) she hides.

1300–1. Cf. 1413–14 and note.

1310. U 'if' (Gdf. 10, 247c).

1327. en danture 'in one's youth'. Mussafia, op. cit., p. 607, and Littré assume this expression derives from *dentatura*. However T.-L. 2, 2027 and F.E.W. 3, 132a realign it with *donteüre*. Cf. Morawski 1765: 'Qu'aprent poulains en denteüre Tenir le veut tant come il dure'; *S. Auban*, ed. A. R. Harden, A.N.T.S. XIX (Oxford, 1968), note on l. 619; *Oxford Dictionary of English Proverbs*, s.v. *trick*, 'The trick the colt gets at his first backing will, while he continueth, never be lacking' (not, however, attested until 1721).

1331. Cf. Introduction, p. xxvi.

1332. en sa chemise 'in her shift', hence 'in herself, without adornment, dowry, etc.'.

1334. **les cerchast** One would expect *le cerchast* (sc. *le munde*), cf. *Erec* 2416, T.-L. 2, 122. Another example where *LOV* appear to have a common error, cf. Introduction, p. xvii.

1358. 'she will look upon you with an unfavourable eye'; cf. Gdf. 10, 227b.

1367–8. If **certein** has its normal sense of 'sure, certain', which seems appropriate in the context, then **car** would have to be taken in the sense of *que* 'that' (cf. *O* and T.-L. 2, 40–1).

1374. A common proverb, Morawski 2159, later used by Beaumont and Fletcher in the *Scornful Lady* II, i, 110–11:

> I will end with the wise man and say
> He that holds a woman has an eel by the tail.

Cf. also M. P. Tilley, *A Dictionary of the Proverbs in England in the Sixteenth and Seventeenth Centuries* (Ann Arbor, 1950) W640.

1393. **les plus devorz** 'most separations, dissensions'. The adjectival use of **plus** would seem to be an Anglicism.

devorz The F.E.W. 3, 110, does not list this development of *divortium*, only *divorce* which is noted as appearing in the fourteenth century.

1398. 'is a real scoundrel, and it is not through her'.

1399. **un chevre** 'a lecherous or lascivious man'. Although the goat's reputation for lechery goes back to antiquity, this is the only occurrence of *chevre* (normally feminine of course) that I have encountered in this context. Neither does *caper* have this attribute. Of the two Latin words *caper* (fem. *capra*) and *hircus*, the former only was retained in French and so the qualities of *hircus* are here transferred to the feminine and generic word *chevre*. T. H. White's *Book of Beasts* (London, 1954), drawing from MS. Cambridge University Library ii.4.26, gives 'HYRCUS, the He-Goat is a lascivious and butting animal who is always burning for coition'. A very early metaphorical use of *hircus* in this sense is found in Plautus' *Mercator* II, ii, 272 ff.:

> Lys: Profecto ego illunc hircum castrari volo,
>   ruri qui vobis exhibet negotium.
> Dem: Nec omen illud mihi nec auspicium placet.
>   quasi hircum metuo ne uxor me castret mea.

1401. **dreit** 'grounds for complaint' (cf. Gdf. 2, 772b).

1404. *Se pener* is usually linked to a following infinitive by *de* (Gdf. 6, 80a).

1413–14. Cf. Morawski 435: 'Cueur de femme est tost mué'.

1419–20. Cf. *Disticha Catonis* I, 12:

> Rumores fuge neu studeas novus auctor haberi;
> nam nulli tacuisse nocet, nocet esse locutum.

1429. **acheisuns** is apparently masculine, though T.-L. 6, 962–7, cites no masculine example. Cf. Introduction, p. xxv.

1433. **repruvez** 'maintain, try to prove', a meaning suggested by Koch which is most convincing in the context.

1441–5. Cf. Seneca (Palmer, op. cit., p. 62):

> *Ratio.* Inuenies si nihil queris nisi bonam. Dum modo ne imagines, proauosque respexeris, nec patrimonium, . . .

1444. **Ke** 'that which'.

1446–8. 'But if one were to take a good look at the woman herself, one would not take her at any price'. For this passage 1443–8, cf. *Disticha Catonis* III, 12:

> Uxorem fuge ne ducas sub nomine dotis,
> nec retinere velis, si coeperit esse molesta.

1449. Koch reads *analee L*, but prints *avale* from *OV*.

1450. **Al mal . . . alee** seems to have the sense of *a mal alé*, 'come to grief', but I have left it because of its appearance in *L* and *V*.

1453. 'for her possessions prevented him from seeing her nature clearly', lit. 'were a visor to him'.

1460. **adevent** is most probably equivalent to *se devient, s'esdevient*, 'perhaps' (T.-L. 3, 1034–5), which fits in well with the sentence as a whole, 1459–61 forming a continuous protasis and 1462 the apodosis.

1468. **U** 'in which'.

1473. 'If you do not keep me in this fashion from now on, . . .'.

1476. 'who will make a bad situation worse for you'.

1491–2. Cf. Theophrastus and St. Jerome (Webb, op. cit., 2, 296):

> Deinde per totas noctes garrulas conquestiones: Illa ornatior procedit in publicum, . . .

1492. **sanz fin** Cf. 865 and note.

1500. 'you do not have the value of a halfpenny in it', i.e. 'you do not own a pennyworth of it'. Cf. A. Tobler, *Vermischte Beiträge* 5 (Leipzig, 1908), 19–23.

1501–2. 'You treat yourself so well with what is mine, that you cannot bear that I should share it'.

1516. **aumosnere** originally meant 'alms-purse' but here means 'purse, bag (attached to the belt)' generally, the whole locution being figurative.

1525. **Si** 'Even if'. One would expect *ne vus poez* as in 951.

1533–4. This couplet also appears in a short collection of proverbs on women in MS. *V*, f. 98r.

1543–4. Cf. Seneca (Palmer, op. cit., p. 58):

> *Sensus.* Amicum perdidi.

1551–2. Cf. Morawski 1357: 'Ne set que pert qui pert son bon ammi'.

1558. **Fors ke** with the indicative, 'except that', here in the looser sense in which it becomes equivalent to 'only, merely': 'you only do so because you please, out of your own perversity'. Cf. the rather similarly 'loosened' sense of *fors* 869.

1559. **Ke** This is probably an adverbial use of the interrogative pronoun, 'why?'.

1569–76. A difficult passage. The idea is that the sea is less treacherous than the world, because its deceptions are at least limited and known, while those of the world may take any form, known or unknown.

1573. Cf. Morawski, *Les Diz*, op. cit., Appendice II, p. 94:

> La grant mer est ce monde cy
> Qui moult est plain de grant soucy.

1582. 'One loyal friend made you secure, reassured you'.

1584. **waucrant** 'sailing, navigating'; cf. 1567–8.

1584–8. Cf. Seneca (Palmer, op. cit., pp. 58–60):

> *Ratio.* Fortem animum habe si vnum, erubesce si vnicum. Quid tu in tanta tempestate ad vnum ancorum stabas.

Note the use of a similar nautical metaphor.

1591–3. 'No matter how many friends you have, you will need them to face the many misfortunes (that will arrive), so that . . .'.

1596. ~ has been transcribed **par. par aventure** = 'perhaps', cf. 773.

1611–14. 'No matter how much you loved him, you would find his match if you had (with the new friend) the friendship and union that was between you (i.e. you and the old friend)'.

1618. 'Some (one or more) of them could be useful to you'.

1630. Cf. note on 787.

1640. Cf. Morawski 171 and *Li Proverbe au Vilain* 72 (ed. A. Tobler, Leipzig, 1895): 'Au besoing voit on qui amis est'.

1641. **de mein en mein** here seems to have the sense of 'of convenience' < *manus*, though T.-L. 5, 823–4, does not give this meaning.

1642. An oft-quoted proverb, Morawski 2283, particularly associated with Lear's Cordelia (Wace, *Brut* 1742).

1645. **deskes en terre** lit. 'down to the ground', hence 'all the way, completely'.

1649. A common proverb, Morawski 215, 216 (also 197) and S. Singer, *Sprichwörter des Mittelalters* (Berne, 1944–7) II, 1, 117; II, 2, 12, the usual full form of which is: 'Au vespre loe on le jor, au matin son oste'.

1650. Cf. *Disticha Catonis* IV, 28:

> Parce laudato; nam quem tu saepe probaris,
> una dies, qualis fuerit, ostendit, amicus.

1657. **de** 'for (the loss of)'.

1687. **adventiz** 'strangers' < *adventicios*. A problem arises from the presence of **issi** where one might expect an adversative 'and yet'.

1699. **menestrel** 'craftsman'; cf. **mester** 1706.

1700. *homo* L is obviously a Latinizing slip.

1714–16. 'This earthly life, which is so bitter according to what you say, is of no other value than making your existence miserable'.

1724. **E** 'and (in addition)'.

1725. **En l'un** i.e. in the original *mesaventure* or the mourning.

1726. **de** *por* would normally be expected after *assez*, but *de* is not uncommon in Anglo-Norman.

1742. 'If they wish to follow the best ideas, the right path'.

1748. From the context one would expect **Fors ke** here to mean 'in order that', but perhaps a closer sense would be 'if I am to have . . .'.

1751. This is unlikely to be the original text. Since the nominative is often *Deu* (27, 42, etc.), one thinks of the possibility of *e Deu l'i mist*. Cf. Introduction, p. xvii.

1751–4. There is some obscurity about the reference of the pronouns **i** 1751 (twice) and **le** 1753 and the subject of **cresse** 1754. It is possible that **i** means 'in me' or 'in what I say' and that **le** refers to **sen**. If **cresse** is 3 sg. of the active verb, 1754 presumably means 'may God increase it (sc. my *sen*)', which fits in well with *e vus si face* 1755, but this does not account for *en ben, en joie e en het* 1754. This line by itself could well mean 'and may I increase in goodness, joy and happiness'. In the context, perhaps we must assume 'may God increase *me*', though the 'me' is not expressed.

1755. '. . . . , and may he do the same for you'.

1761. Koch prints *tute praerie* and gives *ceste* as the variant for *V* only.

TABLE OF PROVERBS

A LINE REFERENCE followed by *n* indicates that the proverb is also treated in the Notes.

A l'envesprer lue l'en [le] jur 1649 *n*
Ausi tost moert li letanz Cum celui ki ad cent anz 173–4 *n*
Ausi vaut meuz morir enfant Ke mut vivere por estre dolent 589–90
Chescune femme devant l'espusaille Mult beal semblant vus fra sanz faille
    1365–6
Cil tent l'anguille dreit par la cue (Ki de mun semblant mult se lue) 1374 *n*
Cum feverer tredze covenant 1298 *n*
Dame Nature, quant vus nasquistes, Tes jurneies ad tutes escrites 357–8
De escufle u de busard Bon ostur averez vus mult tart 837–8 *n*
De la cue feist le chef 301 *n*
Destiné tant a l'enfant si fu De tost morir cum al chanu 613–14
Ennuuse lange e mauveise Quant ne mesdit, n'est pas a eise 849–50 *n*
En plet ne deit aver escut Ki est pendable de tut en tut 815–16
Entremedlez vostre cure De joie u de aukun enveisure 155–6 *n*
En veille gent est li saver 682 *n*
Fetes le ben e ben averez, Si mal vulez, vus en beverez 529–30 *n*
Folie est e grant ennui Mortel pleindre de mor d'autrui 1113–14 *n*
Icil ki vus furma Assez tost vus pestera 907–8
Issi me dune Deu boef par la corne 910 *n*
Ke aprent pulein en danture, L'em dist ke lung tens li dure 1327–8 *n*
Ki ad femme de bone part, Ceo est cheance cum de hasart 1533–4 *n*
Ki cointes est, sages e pruz, Il ert par tut amé de tuz 537–8
Larun ne deit autre juger, Quant il del fet est parcener 817–18
Le lu resemblout le chen (Ne di pas ke tutes teles seient, Nent plus ke
    ceus ki me diseient Ke) 1241 *n*
Le sanc est chaut e le quor leger 685
Meus vaut jofne morir a joie Ke veuz veillard a male voie 227–8
Meuz vaut lesser le gué Ke folement estre bainné 587–8 (345 *n*)
Meuz vaut perdre por estre seur Ke aver de perte tuz jurs pour 1067–8
Moergez vus u u demain, Ne estes pas le premerein 349–50 *n*
N'ad suz cel veillard ne enfant Ke set l'ure del moriant 171–2
N'aviez mie tant de gages Dunt pussez vus coverir les nages (Quant
    entrastes en ceste vie . . .) 893–4 (890 *n*)
Ne tut dire ne tut lesser 1419–20 *n*
Nule perte, ceo savez ben, Vers perte de ami ne ateint a ren 1551–2 *n*
Par tut luist la lune 1257
Perte de ami n'est pas petite 1556
(A mun espeir) Porreit un fol por une pome Fere grant hunte a un
    produme 781–2

Quanke s'e[n] vent, pus s'en revet 317
Quanke vulez, fra le cuntraire Femme, quant serra demaleire 1225–6
Quant vus en estes trop curius, Deus em pensera le meins de vus 939–40 n
Seure chose ad en poverte 903
(Dunc) signefie cest mund la mer 1573 n
Si sages fussez cum Salomon 1626
Si se tent (femme) cum vent en mer, Ore est al west, ore est en le est 1300–1
    (1413–14 n)
Si tost pert le rei sun fiz Cum fet celui ki est mendifs 1123–4 (1119–24 n)
Tant as, tant vaus, e tant vus aim 1642 n
Tant cum l'amez, luez tun chen E ta femme e tun cheval 1280–1
Ta vie n'est fors un pelrimage 362 n
Tun cors est terre e a terre irras 445 n
Tuz avum la lei commune, Les uns le ben, les uns le mal, Le un amuntant
    e l'autre aval 572–4
Un sages hoem e de bel age Suzdure poet un fou curage 441–2
Vent u fumee u nyule en mer Est quor de femme, quant vout amer
    1413–14 n

GLOSSARY

THE glossary is selective, concentrating on words and meanings peculiar to Anglo-Norman and to this text. It excludes words whose meaning and form are the same as, or similar to, Modern French, while several commoner Old French words are also omitted. The most frequent orthographical form is placed first, while the variants included from the manuscripts other than the base are accompanied by the appropriate siglum. The line references are complete save where followed by the sign *etc.*; the letter *n* after a reference indicates that this word appears in a relevant note. Regular verbs are listed under the infinitive, as are all verbs which offer more than one form. The infinitive is followed by a semi-colon if it does not itself occur in the text. Irregular or unusual forms which occur only once and present participles are listed separately. Unless otherwise stated, nouns are listed under the singular oblique form and adjectives under the masculine singular oblique form.

abecé, *s.* learning, schooling 184 |
acheisuns, *sm.pl.* occasions 1429 *n*
achever, *v.n.* end up 1232
acointance, *sf.* close relationship 1613
acoster; *v.refl.* (+ a) place o.s. beside 70
acumpaigner; *v.refl.* associate (a with) 839
acumplie, *pp.f.* finished, ended 555
acuper; *v.a.* accuse 108
adés, *adv.* in plenty 141, (often) enough 767, enough 1270
adevent, *adv.* perhaps 1460 *n*
adulez, *pp.m.sg.nom.* depressed 1064
adventiz, *s.pl.* strangers 1687 *n*
afeitee, *adj.f.* well brought up, educated 1455
affere, *s.* affair, matter 166, 403, 436 *etc.*, disposition 1249
affert, *ind.pr.3* of **afferir,** *v.impers.* be appropriate to, befit 284, 809, 1066
afficher, *v.a.* state, present 162
affit, *s.* affection 1278
age, *sm.* age 604, 684; life 152, 233; **jofne a.** youth 118 *etc.*; **bel a.** middle or old age 116 *n*, 441; **plus entrer en a.** grow older 125; **plus mettre en a.** make older 201
agueitant, *ger.*: **aler a.** watch closely 482
aider 1654; *fut.6* **eiderunt** 204; *subj.pr.3* **ait** 1780; *v.a.* help; *v.refl.* cope 204
amender, *v.a.* improve, change 52, correct 795
ami, *sm.* husband 1404
amie, *sf.* wife 1182, 1213 *etc.*
amuntant, *adv.* up, on top 574

amunter; *v.n.* be of worth 1086 *n*, 1461 *etc.*
anguisse, *s.* pain, anguish 701 *etc.*, *pl.* troubles 203; **por nul a.** at any cost 954 *n*
annuer, *see* **ennuer**
aparceveir; *ind.pr.3* **aparceit** 481, 1353; *fut.6* **aparceverunt** 831; *pp.f.* **aparceue** 1274; *v.a. and refl.* perceive, notice; *pp.* clear 1274
apeau, *ind.pr.1* of **apeler,** *v.a.* call 439
apert, *ind.pr.3* of **apareir,** *v.n.* appear 925
apert: en a. *adv.* uncovered 623, openly 1238
apertement, *adv.* openly 832
aport, *s.* dowry 1458
aprise, *sf.* training, upbringing 1252, 1266 *etc.*
aquassé, *adj.f.* destroyed 1196
arere, *adv.*: **u seit a. u seit avant** sooner or later 618; **mettre a.** set back 200, defeat 958; **sa en a.** before, previously 673, 836 *etc.*
assaer; *v.a.* test 1633
asseur, *adj.* reassured 1540
asseurer, aseurer, *v.n.* be confident (in), rely (on) 1379, 1666; *v.a.* guarantee the safety of 1568
assez, *adv.* enough 697, 908 *etc.*; a lot, plenty 696 *n*, 867 *etc.*; indeed 159, 1612; **de a.** much 672, 771 *etc.*; **plus de a.** much more 1209
assis, *pp. and adj.* provided with, full of 16 *n*, presented, stated 332, placed 1740

ataches, *s. pl.* ribbons 1512

atant, *adv.* then, at that moment 81, 543, 1087

ateint, *ind. pr. 3* of **ateindre,** *v.n.* amount (to) 1552

atrere; ** *ind.pr.3* atret 1697; *fut.3* **atrerra 1362; *v.a.* attract

atur, *sm.* attire, finery 1484

aukes, *adv.* in some measure 370, 876

aumosnere, *sf.* purse, bag 1516 *n*

autresi, *adv.*: **autresi . . . cum** as . . . as 1708

autrui, *pron.* others, other people 33 *n*, 206, 968 *etc.*; property of others 1063, 1064

aval, *adv.* down 574; **la a.** down 1601

avalee, *pp.* gone down, reduced 1449

avant, *adv.* (*place*) **passer a.** pass on 85, 241; *adv.* (*time*) before, previously 266, 1094 *etc.*, henceforth 1297, 1473; *adv.* further 1106, 1541; **en a.** previously 232, henceforth 1166; *see* **arere**

avenir 489 *etc.*; *ind.pr.6* avenent 429 *etc.*; *fut.3* avendrat 949; *subj.pr.3* **avenge** 1479; *pp.* **avenu** 1049; *v.n.* happen; come 949

aventure, *sf.* misfortune 273, 291 *etc.*; **par a.** by chance 23, 469, perhaps 773, 1596

aver, *adj.* miserly, mean 963

averer; *v.a.* show the truth of 1294

aviser, *v.a.* contemplate 78

bacheler, *sm.* husband 1410

bailifs, *s. pl.* governors, magistrates 979

bainer; *ind.pr.5* bainet 103 *n*; *v.refl.* revel 103; *pp.* **bainné** wet, soaked 588

barnage, *sm.* barons, nobles 1130

bataille, *sf.* fuss 1144, argument, debate 1738

beau, *adj.*: **si b. vus est** if that pleases you 243; *see also* **age**

beaut, *adj.* bold, confident 249 *n*, gay 930 *n*

beivre; *ind.pr.3* beit 1631, *6* **beivent** 610; *fut.5* **beverez** 530 *n*; *v.a. and n.* drink; (fig.) 530 *n*, 610; *subst.inf.* drink 989, 1023, 1041

ben, *sm.* good (as opposed to evil) 261, 346 *etc.*, good things 16, 811, 814, wealth 936; *pl.* fine qualities 1189, 1323, 1698

benuree, *adj.* happy 1054

besley, *s.*: **aler a b.** fall into disorder 1132

besturné, *pp.* changed (for the worse) 508

beverie, *s.* heavy drinking, drunkenness 1271

bleste, *sf.* clod of earth 648 *n*

boef, *s. see* 910 *n*

bonement, *adv.* with pleasure 289, in good faith, with kindness 795

busoin, *sm.* need 1306; **en b.** when needed 1652, 1657; **al grant b.** when most needed 1640

cas, *sm.* situation 1072, 1117, incident 1539, 1549

cenele, *sf.* haw; **ne li vaut pas une c.** is not worth a jot to him 970

cert, *adj.* sure, certain 1237

certein, *adj.* sincere 32, sure, certain 1367

chalange, *s.*: **sanz c.** *adv.* without opposition 536

chaleir, *v.impers.* matter 789, 953

changer, *v.refl.* change one's attitude 1014

chanter; *v.a.* proclaim 553

chanu, *adj.* whitened by age 147, 566 *etc.*; *sm.* old man 195, 614

chape, *sf.*: **la c. del cel** the vault of heaven 1303

chapitres, *s. pl.* groups 1396

char, *sf.* body 450

chatel, *sm.* possessions 1453

chaucer, *s.* shoes, footwear 1040

cheance, *s.* luck 1534

cheeir; *ind.pr.3* chet 1110; *fut.6* **cherrunt** 1370; *condit.1* cherreie 146; *pret.3* chei 1513; *pp.* **cheet** 860; *v.n.* fall

chef, *sm.* head 301; **par mun c.** my word 885; **venir a c. de** achieve 1599; *see also* **tur**

cheitif, *adj.* unhappy, miserable 167, 695; *sm.* prisoner 218, unhappy wretch 422, 1200, scoundrel 1505

chemise, *sf.* shift 1332 *n*

chever; *v.n.* end, finish 1178

chevre, *sm.* lecher 1399 *n*

chiche, chice, *V* **chinche,** *adj.* miserly 962, 963

choisir; *fut.5* **choiserez** choose 1440; *pret.3* **choisi** notice 57

ci, si, *adv.* here 12, 43, 101 *etc.*

ciw, *adj.* blind 909

cleime, *ind.pr.3* of **clamer,** *v.refl.* (+ **por**) declare o.s. 1354

cointes, *adj.nom.sg.* clever, wise 537

colees, *sf.pl.* blows 379

coment, cument, *adv.*: **c. ke seit** however it may be, in any event 475, 822 *etc.*

communement, *adv.* together 503

conus, *ind.pr.1* of **conoistre,** *v.a.* know 119

cop, *sm.* blow 380, 756

coveiter; *v.a.* desire 1412

coveitus, *s. pl.* the greedy 35

covenant, *s.* character, attitude 1298 *n*, promise, pledge 1474

coverir, *v.a.* cover 894

cresse, *subj.pr.3* of **creistre,** *v.a.* increase 1245 *n*, 1754 *n*

crewes, *adj.f.pl.* believed 1320

cucher, *subst.inf.* going to bed 209

cue, *sf.* tail 301, 1374 *n*

cum, *adv.* as (in the manner of) 174, 658 *etc.*; how 153, 231; *conj.* as 154, 207, 927, 1124, 1437, than 566; (tant) **c. plus** . . . (tant) **plus, tant c.** . . . **plus** . . . **tant** the more . . . the more 125–6, 1673–4, the longer . . . the more 197–8, 230; **c. plus** . . . **tant** . . . **greinnur** the more . . . the greater 201–2; *see also* **autresi, plus, si, tant**

cunfundre; *v.a.* upset 26, 1180

cunfus, *adj.* troubled 178, 298, 692

cungé, *s.* permission 1171

cunquerre, *v.a.* convert 902; *fut.5* **cunquerrez** conquer 404

cunte, *sm.* situation 1462; **tenir c. de** take into consideration 654

cuntee, *s.* dispute 986 *n*

cuntraire, *sm.* opposite 1225

cuntralier; *v.a.* oppose, be hostile to 515

cuntre, *prep.*: **dire c.** reply to 302, 721, 886; **penser c.** take thought for 906

cuntrové, *pp.* invented 662

cunvenir, *v.n.*: **lesser a c.** let take care of matters 397 *n*, 856

cunverser; *v.n.* dwell 897

cunvoier; *v.a.* escort 1116

curage, corage, *sm.* mind, soul 13, 442 *etc.*; opinion 411, 1417, 1662

cural, *adj.* that wounds the heart 1726

cure, *s.*: **aveir c.** 433, **prendre c.** 1364 (+ **de**) care for, worry about; **mettre en c.** trouble 1032

curent, *ind.pr.6* of **curre,** *v.n.* run 861

curius, *adj.* worried, anxious 939

cursale, *sf.* prostitute 1388

curuz, *sm.* anger 270, 707, act causing anger 1403

custume, *s.* custom 115, 793; **aveir en c.** be accustomed to 834

cutes, *s.pl.* elbows 1488

cuveitise, *sf.* greed 1051

cuvenance, *sm.* performance, fulfilment 1606

cuvenir; *ind.pr.3* **cuvent** 206, 211 *etc.*, **cuveent** 984; *v.impers.* be necessary

cuverture, *s.* pretence 1733

damage, *sm.* harm 202, 527, 1075

dangeruse, *adj.f.* difficult, hard to please 1355

danture, *s.* training period 1327 *n*

danzelant, *ger.*: **aler d.** pamper 208 *n*

deboneire, *adj.* noble, good 1244, 1295

debonerté, *s.* good nature 1689

dechece, *subj.pr.3* of **decheeir,** *v.n.* fail (in health) 605

dedure, *v.a.* entertain 1, amuse 1166

dedut, *sm.* pleasure, amusement 718, 1128, 1265

defors, *adv.*: **mettre d.** exclude 29

dehet, deshet, *sm.* unhappiness 224, 475, 594; **mettre en d.** make unhappy 410

deiz, *sm.pl.* fingers 1511

delit, *sm.* joy, pleasure 103, 198

deliter; *v.refl.* take pleasure 1764

delitius, *adj.* pleasant, enjoyable 9

delivre, *adj.* freed, delivered 1524

demaleire, *adj.* bad 1226, 1243

demande, *sf.* reply to a question 1541

demeine, *adj.* own 1683

demeintenant, *adv.* immediately 1157 *n*

demener; *pres.part.* **demenant** 86; *ind.pr.1* **demein** 1472, *3* **demeine** 230, *5* **demenez** 93, 101; *fut.1* **demenerai,** *V* **demerrai** 466, *6* **demenerunt,** *V* **demerrunt** 1138; *v.a.* display 86, 93, 101 *etc.*, experience 230, lead 466; *v.refl.* be worried, tormented 1138

dementant, *ger.*: **aler d.** lament 428

demorer; *ind.pr.6* **demeorent** *O* 1138; *fut.3* **demorra** 262; *v.n.* remain

depincer; *v.a.* peck 629

deport, desport, *s.* joy, pleasure 312, 1519

derein, drein, *adj.* last 351; *sm.*: **au d.** in the end 363, 1016

descharger; *v.a.* unburden 1007

desclose, *pp.f.* revealed 766

descoverir, *v.a.* reveal 954; *pp.* **descovert** exposed 624

descunfire, *v.a.* destroy 486, defeat 1728

desdire, *v.a.* take away 485, deny 1170

deserte, *sf.* due reward, deserts 859

deservir, *v.a.* deserve 778

deseverance, *sf.* separation 1406

deske, deskes, *adv. and prep.*: **d. a** until 1382, 1520 *etc.*; **d. enz a** right up to 1602; **d. ore** until now 875; **d. en terre** completely 1645 *n*; *conj.* until 1644

desmentir; *v.a.* contradict, give the lie to 1737

despit, *s.*: **tenir en d.** scorn 900

desportant, *ger.*: **s'en aler d.** amuse oneself 109

destre, *adj.* right 1564

destreit, *s.* distress 700

destructiun, *s.* discomfort 665

detrenché, *pp.* hacked to pieces 381

devant, *prep.* *(time)* before 1365; **d. ceo ke** *conj.* before 1062

deveir; *ind.pr.1* **dei** 1732, *3* **deit** 304 *etc.*, *5* **devez** 113 *etc.*, *6* **deivent** 141, 286; *condit.3* **devreit** 1101, 1654, *5* **devriez** 798; *subj.impf.3* **dust** 800, *5* **dussez** 660 *etc.*, **6 dussent** 674, 795 ; *v.n.* must, ought to; have reason to 798 *n*, be sure to 864

devenir 1388 ; *fut.3* **devendra** 1043 *n*; *condit.1* **devendreie** 147 ; *subj.impf.3* **deveneist** 1216 *n*; *pp.* **devenu** 1002 ; *v.n.* become; come 1002

devorz, *s.pl.* separations, dissensions 1393 *n*

devurer; *fut.6* **devurrunt** 630 ; *v.a.* tear to pieces

dez, *s.pl.* dice 1370

dimeine, *sm.* Sunday 186

discretiun, *sf.* judgement 437

dit, *sm.* words 16, 162 *etc.*

doel, *sm.* grief 257; **en d.** grieving 694; **aveir un d.** be sorry 1136

doleir, doler, *see* duleir

doluser, *v.n.* grieve 478, 1340

dous, *num.adj.* two 1018, 1466; **en d. e en treis** 787 *n*, **de d. en treis** 1630 indiscriminately, equally (?)

dreit, *sm.* right, claim 311, 821 *etc.*, right (as opposed to wrong) 1074, grounds, reason 1184, fairness 1260, grounds for complaint 1401 *n*; **par d.** by right 1102, 1732; **a bon d.** rightly so 444; **a tort u a d.** rightly or wrongly 824, 978

dreit, *adj.* straight 1776, true 306, 1352, right 1181, 1482

dreit, *adv.* right 1374

duleir 137 *etc.*, **doleir** 877 *etc.*, **doler** 1184; *ind.pr.1* **doil** 1337, 1563, *5* **dulez** 1675; *imper.5* **dolez** 1173; *v.n. and refl.* grieve, lament; *subst.inf.* grieving, lamentation 402, 541 *etc.*

duner 1172; *ind.pr.3* **dune** 237, 910, 1133; *fut.1* **durrai** 1426, *3* **dorra** 191, 1508; *subj.pr.3* **doint** 42, 54 *etc.*, **doyne** *V* 226, **doine** *V* 1756, **doinst** *V* 1775; *v.a.* give; inspire 1133 *n*; *subst.inf.* giving 1172

dunt, *pron.* about which 366, 1082, because of which 1196, of which 1250; *interr.* how 1264

durer; *ind.pr.3* **dure** 604, 1328; *fut.3* **dorra** 972 *n*; *v.n.* last

dutance, *s.*: **en d.** in doubt 1255

effrei, *sm.* trouble 92

eir, *s.* heir 1101, 1130 *etc.*

eire, *s.* journey through life 1296

el, *adv.*: **par el** by another way 330

empeinte, *sf.* attack 874

empeirer 775, 783 *etc.*; *ind.pr.3* **empire** 1272; *v.a.* defame 775, 783; spoil, harm 1272

emperus, *s.pl.* emperors 354

emprise, *sf.* enterprise, undertaking 252, 486, 1694

encheisun, *sf.* occasion 981, reason 1691 ; **par e. de** because of 988

encumbrer, *v.a.* burden 948, 1246

encumbrer, *s.* difficulty, burden 1574, 1771

encuper, *v.a.* blame, accuse 244

encurra, *fut.3* of **encurre**, *v.a.* catch (illness) 993

encusé, *pp.* blamed 346

endementers, *adv.* meanwhile 724, 1426

endreit, *adv.*: **ci e.** here and now, straight away 879

endurer 965, 1502; *fut.3* **endurra** 104; *v.n.* last 104; *v.a.* bear, endure 965, 1502

enfance, *s.* youth 127, childhood 1680, childishness 1709

enfant, *sm.* young man 3, 85 *etc.*; child 207, 491 *etc.*

engendrure, *sf.* offspring 1080

enginner, *v.a.* deceive 40

engleter, *s.* briar, wild rose 1299 *n*

ennuer, *v.a.* trouble 309, **annuer** irk 881 *n*

ennuuse, *adj.f.* troublesome, unpleasant 849 *n*

enquerrum, *fut.4* of **enquerre**, *v.n.* (+ **de**) examine 1106

enrevere, enrevre, *adj.* malicious 1356, 1400

ensement, *adv.* similarly 631

ensenser; *v.a.* enlighten 547

entasser, *v.a.* pursue 242 (T.-L. 3, 559)

entendement, *s.* intention 801

entente, *sf.* endeavour 113, 1326

enterin, enterrine, *adj.* sincere, loyal 734, 946, 1187

entredalier; *v.refl.* argue, debate 4 *n*

entremedler; *v.a.* intersperse 155

entremettre, *v.refl.* take the trouble to 655

entrepris, *pp.* disturbed 1478, perplexed 1546

enveisee, *adj.f.* gay, good-humoured 1276

enveisure, esveisure, *sf.* pleasure, gaiety 24, 111 *etc.*, pleasing tale 2

envesprer, *s.* evening 1649

erraument, *adv.*: **tut e.** straight away 290, 1034

esbaneer; *v.refl.* amuse oneself 23

eschivre 25; *fut.5* **eschivrez** 1577; *v.a.* escape, avoid

escripture, *s.*: **en e.** written down 603

escrit, *s.* writing, written works 804, scripture 938

escrit, escrite, *pp.* written 153, 235, planned 358

escufle, *s.* kite 837 *n*

escut, *s.*: **aver e.** be listened to 815

esisevelir, *v.a.* L 460 = **ensevelir**

esmaer; *v.refl.* be dismayed, worried 14, 392, 739 *etc.*

espeir, *s.* plaint 1312, expectation 616 *n*; **a mun e.** in my opinion 780
espier, *v.a.* look upon 1547
espine, *s.* briar 1188
esprent, *ind.pr.3* of **esprendre,** *v.a.* inflame 32
espruver; *ind.pr.3* esproeve 733, 736, *5* espruvez 1659; *fut.5* esproverez 738; *pret.5* espruvastes 1652; *pp.* espruvé 266, espruvé 1623, *pl.* espruvez 1644; *v.a.* put to the test; *pp.* experienced 266
espusaille, *s.* wedding 1365
estage, *sm.* state, situation 361
estee, *sm.* summer 68
estencelee, *pp.* dotted 64
ester 245 *etc.*; *pret.3* estut 87; *v.n. and refl.* stand; **lesser e.** let be 245, leave aside 402, 1528
estor, *sm.* furnishings 1490
estrange, *adj.* foreign 415, 435 *etc.*, strange 108; *s.* foreigner 426, 535
estrangement, *adv.* extraordinarily 99
estrif, *sm.* debate, argument 9, 1778
estrus, *s.*: **a e.** completely 745, promptly 1285
estuer; *subj.impf.1* estuasse 216, *3* estuast 1516; *v.a.* keep 1516; *v.refl.* keep o.s. (for) 216
estuper, *v.a.* check, stop 854 *n*
ewe, *sf.* water 58

faillir 325, **failler** 327; *ind.pr.3* faut 582, 1593; *fut.3* faudra 1520, *6* faudrunt 1640; *condit.3* faudreit 1653; *subj.pr.3* faille 748, 750; *v.n.* fail; be wanting 582
fausime, *sf.* falseness, deceit 1246, 1602
feble, *adj.* weak 13, 1219
fei, fai 1565, *sf.* faith, spirit 526; **par f.** in truth 1163, 1254 *etc.*; **en bone f.** in good faith 1672; **porter f. a** place confidence in 769
felunesse, *adj.f.* cruel 292, malicious, pitiless 1238, 1390
fere, *v.a. and refl.* do 207, 224 *etc.*, make, create 164, 189 *etc.*, act 114, cause 202; **f. ke sage** act wisely 179, 1173, 1661; **lesser f.** let be, ignore 835
fes, *sm.* burden 356, 1008; **prendre a f.** take seriously 142, 792
feverer, *sm.* February 1298 *n*
ficher; *v.a.* put 1468
fin, *s.*: **sanz f.** continually 865 *n*, 1492
fine, *adj.f.* noble 945
fiu, *sm.* fief 76
flaelé, *pp.* tormented 728
foer, *sm.*: **a nul f.** in any way 754; **en memes le f.** in the same way 308
folage, *sm.*: **torner a grant f.** consider very foolish 126

fors, *prep.* except 138, 261 *etc.*, only 869; **fors ke** *conj.* provided that 112, 953 *n*, except that, merely 1558 *n*, if 1748 *n*
fors, *adv.*: **fors parti,** O **forparti** excluded 1140 *n*
fortune, *sf.*: **par f.** by misfortune 1058
fous, *s.* fool 1214, 1371; **fous large** 962 *n*; **foularge** 971 spendthrift
franchise, *sf.* nobility of character 1251 *etc.*
fuisun, *s.*: **aver f. (en)cuntre** prevail against 1732; **a grant f.** in great abundance 1330
funtaine, *sf.* spring, stream 57
funz, *s.pl.* depths 1601
furmer; *v.a.* make 907

gages, *s.pl.* pledges, possessions 893
garisse, *subj.pr.3* of **garir,** *v.a.* protect 1770
garnesture, *s.* help 1595 (T.-L. 4, 181-2)
garnir, *v.a.* provide for 1130
gas, *s.*: **sanz g.** seriously 446; **a g.** amusing 562
gent, *sf.* people (*collect.*) 31, 115 *etc.*; people, subjects 1137
gentrise, *sf.* nobility of character 1442
giu parti, gui parti, *sm.* decision 578, end 644
grace, *sf.* blessing 1748, grace 1756; *pl.* thanks 1234, talents, graces 1330
gravele, *sf.* shingle 60, pebble 1192
gré, *s.* thanks 239
gref, *adj.* grievous, painful 382, 477 *etc.*; *sm.* worry 302, 886
grevance, *sf.* troubles 7
grever, *v.a.* harm, hurt 67, 865, 1075 *etc.*
gueres, *adv.* much, to any extent 67, 1231, fully, altogether 1461, long 604; (+ *neg.*) not much, little 829, 1364, (+ **de**) 936, 1765, not long 972; *see also* **pru**
gui, *see* **giu**
guier; *v.a.* guide 400

hardement, *sm.* courage 734
hardiement, *adv.* frankly 1292
hart, *sf.* hangman's rope 1494
hasardur, *s.* prodigal 1148
hasart, *s.* dicing game 1534 *n*
haschee, *s.* affliction 757
haster, *v.a.* hasten 149
haut, *s.*: **mettre en h.** value highly 1283
heiter; *v.a.* please, cheer 75; *pp.* **heité** happy 671
herberger, *v.n.* dwell 686
herneis, *sm.* attire 1465
het, *s.* happiness 1754
hidur, *sf.* horror 667

illurs, *adv.* elsewhere 128
irascu, *pp.* annoyed 625
irruse, *adj.f.* bad-tempered 1365
issi, *adv.* thus 211, 563, 571 *etc.*, and so 711, so 1521
itant, a itant, *see* **tant**

ja, *adv.* indeed, in fact 713, 961, now 1056, 1078; **ja . . . ne** never 47, 50, 190 *etc.*; **ja ren ne** not in any way 592, 730; **ja si . . . ne** 66 *n*, 68 *etc.*; **ja tant ne** no matter how 448, 598, no matter how much 387, 499, 1611, no matter how many 1591 *n*
jangleier; *v.n.* chatter, prate 1302
jofne, *adj.* young 10, 118 *etc.*; *sm.* young man 111, 119 *etc.*
joiir 564, **joier** 1523, *v.n.* rejoice 1523; *v.refl.* (+ de) enjoy 564
jolif, *adj.* gay 124
jolifté, *s.* levity (of character and conduct) 6
jovene, *s.* young man 19
juaus, *s.pl.* jewels 1467
juer, *v.n.* amuse oneself 246, 983, put on an act 1360, 1637
jur, *s.*: **tute jur** any time 489
jurneies, *sf.pl.* days 358
jus, *adv. see* **munt**
juvencel 133, O 21, O 43 *etc.*, **jeovencel** O 73, **jovencel** O 121, *sm.* young man
juvente, *sf.* youth 5 *n*, 114 *etc.*

ke, *rel.pron.* what 1327, 1402, which 1422
keke 567, 1122, 1189 *etc.*, **queke** 1427, O **queyke** 1189 *etc.*, V **queke** 1189, *rel.pron.* whatever
ki, *rel.pron.* those whom 200, he who 237, 327 *etc.*; *conj.* that L 334, L 944

la, *adv.*: **sa e la** here and there, this way and that 55, 177, 208; **de la** on the other side 1594
las, *adj.* wretched, miserable 352, 432 *etc.*
latin, *sm.* intelligence 150 *n*
lebarz, *s.pl.* leopards 640
lede, *adj.f.* unpleasant 627
ledenger; *v.a.* harm 1013
lee, lez, *adj.* happy, gay 158, 1063 *etc.*
leres, *s.* scoundrel, rogue 37 *n*
let, *sm.* insult 826
letanz, *sm.* baby, suckling 173
lettre, *s.* schooling 184
lie, *sf.* integral, unavoidable fault 713 *n*
liu, *sm.* place 75, 659
loin, loinz, *adv.* far 423; **u l. u pres** in any way 375; **e pres e l.** in every way 1305, 1639; **ne pres ne l.** in no way 1658

loreins, *sm.pl.* harness straps 1486
losenger; *v.a.* flatter 1630
lu, *sm.*, **luus,** *pl.* wolf 630, 1241
luer; *ind.pr.1* **lou** 845, 855, *3* **lue** 1373, 1649; *imper.5* **luez** 1280; *v.a.* praise; advise 845, 855; *v.refl.* (+ de) trust 1373

maille, *sf.* halfpenny 1500 *n*; **ne valeir une m.** not to be worth anything 498 *n*, 1318
mal, *adj.* bad, evil 31, 234 *etc.*; **tenir a m.** consider as evil 599; *s.* **sanz m.** without prejudice 1010; **aler al m.** come to grief, end up badly 1450 *n*; **fere de m. le pis** make a bad situation worse 1476 *n*
maleisun, *sf.* curse 42, 1508
malement, *adv.* badly, evilly 1138
manere, *sf.* way 762, 1020 *etc.*, kind 1316, nature 199, 1350; **en tute m.** in all ways 957; **de meinte m.** in great variety 69 *n*; **en meinte m.** in many ways 1000
mangue, *ind.pr.3* of **manger,** *v.a.* eat 1631
marrement, *sm.* affliction 100
marri, mari, *adj.* grieved 366, 976
martyre, *s.* suffering, torment 776
mascher; *v.a.* chew 1517
maubailli, *pp.* destroyed 1018; **de quor m.** heart-broken 1202
mautalent, *sm.* dejection, despondency 84
mein, *s.*: **de m. en m.** of convenience 1641 *n*
meintenir 934, 1774; *ind.pr.6* **meintenent** 694; *imper.5* **meintenez** 1661; *subj.pr.3* **meintenge** 1480, 1753; *v.a.* keep, retain; maintain, support 1480, 1753; *v.refl.* support o.s. 934
memorie, *s.* mind 800
mendifs, *s.* beggar 1124
menestrel, *sm.* craftsman 1699 *n*
mentir; *v.n.* be mistaken 1440
menuement, *adv.* into small pieces 381
merci, *s.* thanks 239, thank you 871; **vostre m.** by your leave 705, 1749
mesaffeité, *adj.* bad-tempered 1531
mesaventure, *sf.* misfortune 434, 583 *etc.*
meschef, *sm.* disaster 558, 1004
meseise, *sf.* wretchedness 569
meseisee, *adj.* wretched 869
mesestance, *sf.* troubles 8, calamity 1710
mesfetes, *ind.pr.5* of **mesfere,** *v.n.* do wrong 888
mesquider; *v.n.* be mistaken 911
mester, *s.* craft, skill 1706; **aveir m. de** need 120, 1125, 1204 *etc.*; **aveir m.** 1590, 1618, **i aveir m.** 1592 be necessary

mestre, mettre *L* 680, *sm.* master, teacher 121, 540 *etc.*, victor 743, master, craftsman 1703

mestrie, *sf.* mastery, victory 1730

mesure, *sf.* moderate words 408, moderation 584, 774

mettre, *v.a.* put 656 *etc.*, pit 845; instruct (**a** in) 183 *n*, impute (**sur** to) 777; *v.refl.* (+ **en**) enter 46; *see also* **arere, cure, defors, dehet, nunchaleir, resun**

meuz, *sm.*: **fere mun m.** better myself 470; **se tenir al m.** *see* 1742 *n*

mor, *s.* death 1114

moriant, muriant, *sm.* the moment of death 172, 420

morir 136, 139 *etc.*; *ind.pr.1* **moer** 193, **moerc** 421 *n, 3* **moert** 173, 611; *fut.1* **morrai** 296 *etc.*, *3* **morra** 329, 391, *5* **morrez** 343, 369, **morrer** 364; *pret.6* **morirent** 354; *subj.pr.1* **moere** 465, *3* **moerge** 1152, *5* **moergez** 349, 443; *pp.* **mors** 968, 1103, **mort** 447 *etc.*, *f.* **morte** 1195, 1337; *v.n.* die

moveir; *ind.pr.3* **meot** 313, **moet** 328, 1304, *6* **moevent** 1396; *pret.3* **mut** 1088; *v.a.* move 1396, upset 313, turn 1088; *v.refl.* move 1304, get upset 328

mun, *adv.* indeed 275

mund, munde, *sm.* world 248, 384 *etc.*, earthly life 25, 49 *etc.*

munt, *adv.*: **m. e jus** up and down 177 *n*

munter; *v.n. see* 712 *n*

murdrir, *v.a.* conceal 1027 *n*

murne, *adj.* sad 83, 175, 1338

murs, *sf.pl.* manners 1323

musage, *sm.* wasting time 151, 180

musardie, *s.* stupidity 457, 534; **fere m.** be foolish 215

mustrer, *v.a.* reveal 7, 294 *n*

mustresun, *sf.* finery 1489

nages, *s.pl.* buttocks 894

naive, *adj.f.* natural 78

naturesce, *s.* simplicity 1252

neez, *pp.pl.* drowned 639

neis, *adv.* not even 511

nekedent, *adv.* however 335, 1257

nent, nept *L* 1240, *adv.*: **n. plus** (+ *neg.*) no more 1586, 1715, 1727, **n. plus ke** no more than 1240

neporoek, *adv.* none the less 1429

nestre, *subst.inf.* birth 608

nette, *adj.f.* pure 59, 946

noise, *sf.* babbling 61

nomer; *v.a.* mention 295, 1094, call 304

nuanz, *adj.m.pl.* swimming 924

nue, *sf.* sky 1229

nunchaler, *s.*: **mettre en n.** pay little heed to 221

nunpoier, *s.*: **cheeir en n.** become weak 146; **mettre enz n.** make powerless 742

nunsavant, *adj.* ignorant 687

nunsaveir, *s.* ignorance 213

nut, *s.* night 702, 717

nyule, *s.* fog, mist 1413

oes, *s.*: **a oes** for the benefit of 968

oil, *sm.* eye 1358 *n*, 1564

orfreiz, *sm.pl.* gold embroidering 1512

orgoiller; *v.refl.* be vain (**de** about) 1458

oscire, *v.a.* kill 916

ost, *s.* battle 752

ostur, *sm.* hawk 838 *n*

otreier; *v.a.* grant, concede 680

pais, *sm.* country 415, 423 *etc.*, home 518

paisant, *sm.* countryman 1141

papelarz, *s.pl.* hypocrites 35

paraler, *sm.*: **au p.** in the end 1390, 1638

parcener, *sm.* participant 818

pareir; *ind.pr.3* **pert** 94, 102 *etc.*; *ind.impf.3* **pareit** 84; *v.n.* appear 84, 1762; *v.impers.* be manifest 94, 102, 923

parent, *s.* kinsman 512 *n*

part, *sf.* direction 82, 502 *etc.*, share 370, provision for the future 1096; **de bone p.** of a good family 1533

passer, *v.a.* pass 85, 297 *etc.*, pass beyond 360, 597, surpass 584, 1188 *etc.*, outdo, defeat 698

pautener, *sm.* rogue 1126

pé, *sm.* foot (*measure*) 404 *n*

peissuns, *s.pl.* fish 924

pelrimage, *sm.* journey 362, 412, 436

pendable, *adj.* deserving of hanging 816

pener; *v.refl.* worry (**de** about) 791, 1035 *etc.*, take the trouble 786

pensé, pensee, *sm.* worry 548, 1072

penser; *v.n.* think 160 *etc.*, worry 130, 395 *etc.*, wonder 377; *subst.inf.* thought 22, 39, *etc.*, worry 145, 276 *etc.*

per, *sm. and f.* equal 1389, 1424, 1612

peresce, *s.* indolence 6

pes, *sf.* peace of mind 1478

pesa, *adv.* long ago 1097

pesantume, *s.* misery 1712

pestera, *fut.3* of **pestre,** *v.a.* feed 908

petit, *adv.* little 899; **mult p.** a very short time 104, very little 1720; *sm.* a little 484, a small matter 998

pincer; *v.a.* extort money from 980

plaé, *pp.* wounded 388

pleggage, *s.* guarantee 187

plegges, *s.pl.* guarantors 984

pleidur, *sm.* litigant 38 *n*

pleinte, *sf.* misfortune 862, plaint 954

pleisir; *ind.pr.3* **plest** 223 *etc.,* **plet** 288; *fut.3* **plerra** 1150; *condit.3* **plerreit** 699; *subj.pr.3* **place** 882, 918; **pleise** 523, 567; *v.n.* please; *subst.inf.*: **dire vostre p.** say what you wish 704; **a p.** to one's liking 267

plet, *sm.* debate, discussion *title,* 11, 1396, noise 318, lawsuit 815, 986; **tenir p.** 286, (+ **de**) 476 *etc.,* **rendre p.** 50 *n* heed, pay attention to; **fere bon p.** do s.o. a good turn 825

plus, *adj.* most of 1393 *n; adv.:* **de p.** more 192 *n;* **le p.** all the more 943 *n;* **ne ... plus ... cum** no more than 564; *see also* **cum**

plusur, *pron.* most people 610; **plusurs,** *adj.* 392, *pron.* 580 many

poeir, *s.* wealth 1480, capacity 1773

poet cel estre, *adv.* perhaps 414, 994, 1653

poi, *adv.* little 250, 1030, hardly 1514, not very 102; **poi (de)** little 548, 1234, 1388

pome, pumme 1530, *sf.* trifle 781, 1530, apple 1110

pomer, *sm.* apple-tree 1108

porchaser 1406; *pp.* **porchacee** 1128, **porchacé** 1690; *v.a.* obtain

porquerrunt, *fut.6* of **porquerre,** *v.a.* seek 981

porteure, porture, *s.f.* offspring 407, bearing, behaviour 1441

porveance, *s.* provision 941

porveeir; *ind.pr.3* **porveit** 919; *fut.3* **porverrat** 927; *subj.impf.3* **porveist** 914; *pp.* **porveu** 677, 1097; *v.a.* provide 914, 919 *etc.,* ordain 677

poture, *sf.* food 919

pour, *s.* fear 1068, 1670

praerie, *sf.* meadow 1262, 1761

preiser 1720; *ind.pr.3* **prise** 1283; *v.a.* value 899, 1720, value highly 898, 1275, 1283

premerein, *adj.* first 350

pres, *adv. see* **loin**

proeme, *s.* neighbour 40, 826

proie, *sf.* property 1471 (F.E.W. 9, 286a)

pru, *s.* profit, benefit 964; *adv.:* **gueres pru** (+ *neg.*) not very well 204

prudum 263, 315 *etc.,* **prudom** 107, 161, **prudome** 658, **produme** 782, **pruedom** 90, **prudume** 1535, *sm.* good man, worthy man 263, 315, 331 *etc.;* **sire p.** good sir 90, 107 *etc.*

pulein, *s.* colt 1327

putre, *adj.* foul 1495

puur, *sf.* stench 626, 666, 669

quanke, *rel.pron.* whatever 34, 118, 163 *etc.,* as much as 347

queke, *see* **keke**

quens, *s.* count 80

querre; *ind.pr.3* **quert** 810, 1021; *imper.5* **querez** 1435, 1659; *pret.1* **quis** 1739; *v.a.* seek 1021, 1435 *etc.,* require 810

quites, *adj.* free (**de** of, from) 316, 456

quor, *sm.* heart 30, 48, 79 *etc.,* inclination 307

rage, *s.:* **turner a r.** become irritated with 117

reaume, reame, *sm.* kingdom 1132, 1263

recoper; *v.a.* cut short 1296

record, *sm.* testimony 823, memory 1003, story 1073 (F.E.W. 10, 160b)

recorder; *v.a.* repeat 1507

recuillir 506, 764, 1198; *ind.pr.3* **recuilt** 534; *v.a.* accept 506, receive 534, admit 764, 1198

redoter; *v.n.* talk nonsense 213

redutee, *pp.* feared 303, 755

regard, *s.:* **fere r.** pay attention 1658

reisun, *see* **resun**

remaneir; *ind.pr.3* **remeint** 532; *pp.* **remis** 646, 718, 1545; *v.n.* dwell 532, rest, remain 646, 718, 1545

remembrance, *s.* memory 1100

ren, *sf.* thing 25, 325, 521 *etc.,* anything 285, 749 *etc.;* (+ *neg.*) nothing 18, 164 *etc.;* **tute ren** all creatures 935; **ne ... de ren** in no way 1359, 1767

renun, *sm.* reputation 783, gossip 789

repeirer; *v.n.* return 363

repruver, *s.:* **en r.** as a reproach 368, in proverb 681, 1420

repruver; *v.a.* maintain, try to prove 1433 *n,* reproach 1469

requerre; *imper.5* **requerez** 1769; *pp.* **requis** 386; *v.a.* ask, request

resembler; *v.n.* seem 1092

respit, *sm.* respite 190, wise saying 15, 332; **aver r.** take as a maxim 236

resun, reisun, *sf.* reason, cause 137, 1557, words 544, 881, 1719, (faculty of) reason 957, what is reasonable 1260 *etc.;* **par r.** with reason 1029, 1059, 1692; **mettre a r.** speak to, guide 438

resusciter; *v.a.* bring back to life 1560

ret, *s.* accusation 108

retter; *v.a.* blame (a upon) 528

retur, *s.* recovery 716

revet (s'en), *ind.pr.3* of **s'en raler,** *v.refl.* go away again 317

rire; *v.n.* smile (at) 1637

rivere, *sf.* river bank 70

rouleer; *v.a.* roll 60

runde, *sf.:* **a la r.** around about 1334

runz, *adj. nom.sg.m.* round, plump 930

rustes, *adj. f.pl.* tattered, in rags 1487

sa, *adv.* 55, 177 *etc.*, *see* **arere, la**; **de sa** on this side 1593

sage, *see* **fere**

saives, *adj.nom.sg.m.* wise 122

sarmoner, *v.n.* preach 182

saver 275, 660, 1608, **saveir** 1598, *v.a.* know 44, 105 *etc.*, learn 191, 235 *etc.*; *v.impers.* please 883; (+ *inf.*) know how 162, 182 *etc.*; *subst.inf.* wisdom 20, 334 *etc.*, wise action 401; **tenir a s.** consider wise 542

scient: a s. deliberately 1109

secle, *sm.* world, earthly life 142, 565, 1544

seer 91; *condit.1* **serreie** 269; *pret.3* **sist** 77; *v.n. and refl.* sit down

seet, *imper.5* of **estre**, *v.n.* be 1237

sei, *s.* thirst 863, 905

sein, *adj.* pure 58, healthy 714, robust 1485

semblant, *sm.* pretence 1218, 1236 *etc.*, appearance 1371, 1373, 1621

senez, *adj.nom.sg.m.* sensible 102

sens, sen, *sm.* good sense, intelligence 214, 250, 321 *etc.*, thoughts 106, manner 160

servir, *v.a.* look after 206, 212

sesun, *s.*: **de s. de** of an age to, ready to 138

sevrer, *v.a.* separate 450

si, *conj.* and 9, 11, 17 *etc.*, as, so *introducing wish* 98, 248 *etc.*; *adv.* thus 114, 300 *etc.*, so 65, 66, 79 *etc.*; **e si** and moreover 1055; **si cum**, *conj.* as 223, 848, 1192 *etc.*; **si . . . cum** as . . . as 311, 454, 461

si, *see* **ci**

signefier, *v.a.* represent 1573

solacer, *v.a.* console 275, 1203

solaz, solas, *sm.* comfort, relief 13, 335 *etc.*, amusement, pleasure 120, 1519

soleir; *ind.pr.1* **soil** 1338; *ind.impf.6* **soleient** 474; *v.n.* be accustomed to

succurs, *s.* help 1594

suef, *adv.* delicately 448, peacefully 461, 1523, sweetly 1361

suffrir 763, 1723; *ind.pr.3* **seofre** 720, **soefre** 739; *pret.3* **suffri** 371, 1684; *v.a.* suffer, bear 371, 720 *etc.*; *v.n.* suffer 739

sujur, sojur, *sm.*: **aver s.** dwell, stay 48, 258; **a gref s.** for an unhappy period 220 *n*

sul, *adj.* alone 46, 869 *etc.*, single 229; *sm.* a single person 1039; *adv.* only 662, 1271

summe, *sf.* the whole story 719, 1016

sur, sure, *adv.*: **curre s.** rush upon 861; **crier s.** shout at 1493

surmunter; *v.a.* conquer 726

surquidez, *adj.* arrogant 519, 772; *sm.pl.* the arrogant 36

surse, *sf.* waters 59, 78

survenir; *v.n.* come along 81

survenue, *s.* arrival 305

sus, *adv.*: **la s.** on high 944; **la sus . . . la val** up . . . down 1308

susprent, *ind.pr.3* of **susprendre**, *v.a.* catch up with 116

sutif 22, 37 *etc.*, **sutil** 249, *adj.* ingenious, clever 22, 249, pleasing, delicate 61; *sm.* cunning person 37

suventefeiz, *adv.* very often 20

suzdure, *v.a.* lead astray 442

talent, *sm.* will, desire 336, 1746

tant, itant, *adv.* so much 130, 132, 144 *etc.*, so 83, 143, 167 *etc.*, so long 1093, a good deal 4; (+ *neg.*) as much 80, sufficient 893; **t. cum** as long as 361, 1646, 1758, as much as 1193, 1280; **de t. cum** as long as 1588; **de t.** to that extent 1014; **de t. ke** inasmuch as 492; **a itant** thereafter 1542; **fors . . . itant ke** except inasmuch as 1271; **ne t. ne quant** at all 1372, 1634; **t. cum plus, cum plus . . . t.** *see* **cum**

tantost, *adv.* at once 560, 1302

tart, *adv.*: **mult t.** never 838; *see also* **tost**

tecche, *s.* spot, trace 1289

temprer; *v.a.* moderate 1417

tenir 398 *etc.*; *ind.pr.1* **teng** 169 *etc.*; *subj.pr.1* **tenge** 819, *5* **tengez** 1473; *v.a.* hold 274, 398 *etc.*, keep 715, maintain 1473; **t. a** consider 169, 542 *etc.*; *v.n.* refrain 1525 *n*; *v.refl.* stop 479, remain 480, 1324, refrain 951, behave 1300, consider oneself 1407; **se t. a** be left with 1452; **se t. al meuz** *see* 1742 *n*; *see also* **despit, plet, saver**

tens, *sm.* time 322, occasion 159, 580; **par t.** early 1152, 1522

tenser, *v.a.* look after 51 *n*

tere; *ind.pr.3* test 884, 1302; *pret.3* **tut** 1087; *v.refl.* be silent

tolir 45, 558 *etc.*; *ind.pr.3* **tout** 414, 768, **toust** 1167; *fut.1* **toudrai** 1678, *3* **toudra** 989; *v.a.* take away 414, 558 *etc.*, get rid of 45, 1678; *subst.inf.* taking away 1172

tort, *see* **dreit**

tost, *adv.* quickly, early, soon 139, 555, 563, 628, 1245 *etc.*; **mult t.** 147, 148, **ben t.** 621 easily, probably; **plus t.** sooner, rather 1199; **ausi t. . . . cum** 173, **si t. . . . cum** 1123, as quickly as; **t. u tart** 326, 369 sooner or later; **e t. e tart** day and night 501, 1493

travail, *sm.* torment 1574

travailler; *v.a.* cause torment 1571; *pp.* **travillee** tormented 985

tredze, *num.adj.* thirteen 1298 *n*

treis, *num.adj.* three, *see* **dous**

tresor, *sm.* treasure room 1027
trespas, *sm.* transgression 796
tresturner; *v.n.* turn 507
tretiz, *sm.* tale 12
tricheres, *sm.* prevaricator 38 *n*
tristur, *s.* sadness 27, 254, 710
tucher; *v.n.* (+ **de**) refer to, speak of 43 *n*
tur, *s.*: **a chef de t.** in the end 195, 619 *etc.*
turner, torner, *v.a.* turn 571, 578, direct 106, 128; *v.n.* **t. a** change to 131; *see also* **folage, rage**
tus, *sm.* young man 10 *n*
tut, *adj.* all 39, 140 *etc.*; **par t.** all over 1511; *indef.pron.* everything, all 399, 505 *etc.*; **de t. en t.** completely 816; **par t.** everywhere 538, 539, 1257; **tuz** all men 376; *sm.* the whole, everything 296; **del t.** completely 960; *adv.* completely, quite 28, 46, 184 *etc.*; (+ *subj.*) although 681, 830 *etc.*

u, *conj.* or 8, 32, 156 *etc.*
u, *adv.* where 132, 293 *etc.*, if 1310 *n*; **u ke** wherever 443, 507 *etc.*
u, *see* **ui**
uelement, *adv.* equally 283
ui, u, *adv.* today 349, 1496
urs, *s.pl.* bears 640
usage, *s.* habits, behaviour 234
user, *v.a* use 345, 1039, practise 836
ut, *num.adj.* eight 1127
utrage, *s.* offence, outrage 1174, insult 1418

vaillant, *ger.*: **aveir v.** have (the value of) 1500 *n*
val, *see* **sus**

veintre 958; *ind.pr.3* **veint** 1020, 1029, 1033, *5* **venkés** 745; *fut.3* **venquira** 746, 1046; *pp.* **vencuz** 751; *v.a.* overcome
veir, *s.*: **dire v.** be right 187, 615 *etc.*
ventage, *sm.* trifle 14 *n*
verdur, *sm.* greenness 71
verraiz, verrais, *adj.m.pl.* true 15, 1629
vers, *prep.* in comparison with 1086, 1552
vesture, *s.* clothes 1040
vif, *adj.*: **be born 168**
vigerus, *adj.* robust 576
vilein, *adj.* nasty, unpleasant 1462; *sm.* wretch, scoundrel 1495
vileinie, vilanie, *s.* maliciousness 271, 707
vis, *sm.* countenance 84
viscuntes, *s.pl.* steward, sheriff 979
visere, *s.* visor, *hence* screen 1453 *n*
vistes, *adj.nom.sg.m.* agile 576
vitaille, *s.* victuals 914
vivant, *sm.*: **en mun v.** in my lifetime 1348
voie, *sf.* path 1115, condition 996; **a male v.** 228, **en male v.** 1392 in a sad state; **en nule v.** in any way 1197
volage, *s.* levity, foolishness 1065 *n*; *adj.* flighty 1377
volunters, *adv.* gladly 723, 1425
vuleir, *subst.inf.* will, desire 510, 1558; **dire sun v.** say what one wants, speak one's mind 278

wandelarz, *s.pl.* swindlers 979 *n*
wanelaces, *s.pl.* treacheries 1233 *n*
waucrant, *adj.* navigating 1584 *n*
west, *sm.* west 1301
wrec, *s.*: **en w.** destitute, in penury 921 *n*

INDEX OF PROPER NAMES

Augustin, seint 799 *n*, St. Augustine

Catun 154, Dionysius Cato, author of the *Disticha*

Deu, 27, 42, 51 *etc.*, **Deus** *nom.* 940, 1245, 1751, **Dé** 727, 1107, 1176, God

Engleis, *sg.* 1279 Englishman

Engletere 1256, 1262, 1264, England

Fortune 571, 1007 Fortune, Destiny

France 1256, 1258, France

Gregoire, seint 799 *n*, St. Gregory

Inde 453 *n*, India

Jesu 391 *n*, Jesus Christ

Marie, seinte 514, 1769, 1780, the Virgin Mary

Mors, *pl.* 453, Moors

Nature 306, 307, **Dame N.** 357 Nature, Mother Nature

Pere, seint 1536, 1729, St. Peter

Pol, seint 797, St. Paul

Richer, seint 299, St. Riquier

Rume 1536, Rome

Salomon 1626, Solomon